Audiovisual Policies
in College Libraries

CLIP Note #14

Compiled by

Kristine Brancolini
Head of Media Services
Indiana University Libraries
Indiana University
Bloomington, Indiana

ASSOCIATION OF
COLLEGE
& RESEARCH
LIBRARIES

College Library Information Packet Committee
College Libraries Section
Association of College and Research Libraries
A Division of the American Library Association

ASSOCIATION OF
COLLEGE
& RESEARCH
LIBRARIES
A DIVISION OF THE
AMERICAN LIBRARY ASSOCIATION

Published by the Association of College and Research Libraries
A Division of the American Library Association
50 East Huron Street
Chicago, IL 60611-2795
312-280-2515
Toll-free 1-800-545-2433 ext. 2515

ISBN: 0-8389-7495-3

The paper used in this publication meets the minimum requirements of American National Standard for Information Sciences—Permanence of Paper for Printed Library Materials, ANSI Z39.48-1984. ∞

Printed in the United States of America.

324340

TABLE OF CONTENTS

CLIP NOTES COMMITTEE

Jonathan D. Lauer, Chair
Messiah College

Dan Bedsole
Randolph-Macon College

James Cubit
Williams College

Ray English
Oberlin College

Victoria Hanawalt
Reed College

Andrea Hoffman
Wheelock College

INTRODUCTION

The CLIP (College Library Information Packet) Notes program of the College Libraries Section of the Association of College and Research Libraries (ACRL) provides college and small university libraries with information and documentation on library practices and procedures. The purpose of the program is "to share information among smaller academic libraries as a means of facilitating decision making and improving performance" (Morein, 1985, p. 226). Each CLIP Note publication includes a summary of survey results describing current practices regarding a particular topic and a selection of documents.

Statement of Purpose

In 1987 the ACRL Audiovisual Committee completed a major project, publication of new "Guidelines for Audiovisual Services in Academic Libraries" (C&RL News, October 1987, 533-536). Now that the guidelines have been adopted and published, how can the committee help academic libraries follow them? As members of the 1988/89 committee discussed new projects that we might undertake, the question of audiovisual policies arose. Those of us on the committee noted that as one writes and revises policies -- collection development, selection, weeding, and circulation -- it is useful to have policies adopted by peer institutions to use as examples or models. However, there are few published examples of such policies. In a recent search of Library Literature (December, 1984, through March 31, 1990) we found no sample policies and only one article on the topic of collection development policies (Dudley, Claire C., "Microcomputer software collection development," Choice, January, 1986, 704-705).

The members of the 1988/89 and 1989/90 ACRL Audiovisual Committees believed that it would be valuable to collect audiovisual policies from academic libraries of all sizes and types. We plan to use an identical survey instrument, so we can compare information across sizes and types of academic libraries. Our first survey resulted in this CLIP Note. A second survey using a slightly altered form of the questionnaire resulted in a SPEC (Systems and Procedures Exchange Center) Kit published by the Association of Research Libraries in December 1990, Audiovisual Policies in ARL Libraries (Kit 162, March 1990). We hope that this CLIP Note will provide valuable comparative information to librarians building audiovisual collections and planning and improving services. We further hope that the documents selected for inclusion provide a variety of policies that other college librarians can use as samples to be adapted to local circumstances.

1

Survey Procedure

Pre-survey planning involved members of both the 1988/89 and 1989/90 Audiovisual Committees. Charles Forrest, Emory University, drafted a sample questionnaire that was reviewed and edited by the entire committee. Kristine Brancolini, Indiana University, drafted a proposal to accompany the questionnaire to be sent to the CLIP Notes Committee of the College Libraries Section of ACRL. The proposal was reviewed by the Audiovisual Committee before it was submitted to the CLIP Notes Committee. Kristine Brancolini conducted the survey and compiled the documents. Robert Danford, Hartwick College, reviewed a selection of the documents and made suggestions for inclusion and exclusion.

The CLIP Notes program uses a pre-established sample of libraries that have agreed to respond to surveys and provide documents (Morein, 1985). The college and small university libraries included in the sample represent two groups from the Carnegie Council on Policy Studies in Higher Education. These are: 1) Comprehensive Universities and Colleges I, and 2) Liberal Arts Colleges. Institutions with a minimum of 1,000 students and a maximum of 5,000 students were sent a questionnaire which asked whether they would be willing to respond to future CLIP Note surveys and share relevant documents. In November 1989, the survey was distributed to the 258 libraries in this sample. Approximately two weeks after the survey was distributed, a second copy of the survey was sent to institutions that had not yet responded.

Survey Results

A total of 155 full-length surveys was returned, for a 60% response rate. The survey data were compiled using Lotus 1-2-3. The survey results and report were sent to all members of the 1989/90 ACRL Audiovisual Committee for comments and suggestions before they were submitted to the CLIP Notes Committee.

At the suggestion of the CLIP Notes Committee, the compiler attempted to gather more documents for the publication by sending out a shorter, follow-up survey to nonrespondents. The follow-up survey was sent to 109 libraries; 52 were returned, for a 48 percent response rate. However, combining the responses to the first and second surveys yields an overall response rate of 78 percent. The following discussion of results does not include the results from the follow-up survey, but the results themselves are reported on pages 13-14.

Audiovisual Collections (Questions 1, 2 and 3)

Of the responding libraries, 148 (95%) have audiovisual collections. These collections range in size from 60 to 157,721 pieces or items. The largest collection includes 140,949 slides. The next largest collection totals 91,800 items. There appears to be no relationship among number of students, size of total collection, and size of audiovisual collections, although this assertion is supported by a visual examination of the data only. It has not been tested statistically.

Respondents reported 23 types of audiovisual materials in their collections. The most popular formats included audiocassettes (86%), audio compact discs (49%), computer software (51%), phonodiscs (82%), slides/slide sets (72%), filmstrips (70%), kits (61%), motion pictures (63%), and videocassettes (86%). No other format is collected by more than 18% of the libraries in the sample.

Purposes of the Audiovisual Collection (Question 4)

Of the 148 libraries that have audiovisual collections, 143 (97%) support classroom instruction, 109 (74%) support individual student use, 59 (40%) support research, 77 (52%) support staff training, and 42 (28%) support the general public. Most respondents who reported that their collections support research indicated that this was done by maintaining archival collections of audio recordings of campus events and lectures.

Although the second part of question #4 asked for responses from libraries that answered "no" to all of the purposes mentioned above, others also answered the question. Nine libraries reported that their campus has an audiovisual center or media department that acquires audiovisual materials. In some cases this campus unit is the sole repository of audiovisual materials on campus; in other cases, this campus unit supplements collections in the library. Nine libraries reported that the campus unit has responsibility for audiovisual equipment, while the library has responsibility for audiovisual materials.

Staffing for Audiovisual Services (Question 5)

Of the 148 libraries with audiovisual collections, 69 (47%) reported having a separate staff for managing audiovisual materials. Of these 69 respondents, 56 (81%) have staff involved in selection, 48 (70%) have staff involved in acquisitions, 51 (74%) have staff involved in budget management, and 69 (100%) have staff involved in public service.

Expenditures for Audiovisual Materials (Questions 7, 8, and 9)

Of the 148 libraries with audiovisual collections, 89 (60%) have a separate fund set aside for acquiring audiovisual materials. The median expenditure for audiovisual materials in libraries with a separate audiovisual fund is more than double the median expenditure for audiovisual materials in libraries without a separate audiovisual fund: $6,000 versus $2,750. The maximum amount spent for audiovisual materials in a library with a separate audiovisual fund is $55,584; the maximum amount spent for audiovisual materials in a library without a separate audiovisual fund is $20,000.

Of the 148 libraries with audiovisual collections, 66 (45%) reported additional sources of funding for audiovisual materials. The most frequent sources mentioned include academic departments -- 15 (10%); book funds -- 9 (6%); donations of materials and gift money -- 25 (17%); and grants -- 23 (16%).

Alternative Methods of Acquiring Audiovisual Materials (Question 10)

Of the 148 libraries with audiovisual collections, 77 (52%) acquire audiovisual materials in at least one way other than purchasing pre-recorded materials. These alternatives include leasing audiovisual materials (39; 26%), purchasing site or blanket licenses (46; 31%), and videotaping off-air or off-satellite (77; 52%). Thirty libraries (20%) reported entering into other similar agreements. The "similar agreements" mentioned are consortium participation (4), purchasing duplication rights (1), and film/video rental (15).

Audiovisual Policies (Questions 11, 12, 13, 14, 15, and 16)

Few libraries with audiovisual collections have policies describing the collections. Eleven libraries (7%) have a separate written collection development policy for audiovisual materials. Twelve libraries (8%) have a written selection policy for audiovisual materials. Four libraries (3%) have a written weeding policy for audiovisual materials.

However, most responding libraries had policies for various aspects of their user services. One-hundred twenty-three libraries (83%) have special circulation policies or limitations on the circulation of audiovisual materials. Ninety-three libraries (60%) operate an audiovisual reserve service. Thirty libraries (19%) charge a user fee for audiovisual collections or services. The only fees mentioned by more than one library were fees for production services and materials, and equipment fees for non-affiliated groups using college or university equipment on or off campus. A complete list of collections or services for which user fees are charged is included in the following summary of results.

4

Documents

Of the 201 libraries that responded to the <u>CLIP Note</u> survey and the follow-up survey, 63 enclosed documents -- 55 libraries from the first survey and 8 libraries from the follow-up survey. Documents from 13 libraries were selected for inclusion. Arranged by library, the types of documents include internal policies and procedures distributed to library staff, external policies and procedures distributed to users, forms to request materials and services, and brochures.

The documents are arranged alphabetically by name of college. Under each college documents are arranged in order received; this arrangement preserves logical order. An index follows the survey summary and provides access to documents by topic.

References

Morein, Grady. (1985). What is a CLIP Note? <u>C&RL News,</u> <u>46</u>, 226-229.

CLIP NOTE SURVEY ON AUDIOVISUAL POLICIES

Directions: All figures requested are for **fiscal year 1988/89.**
If you supply figures from another time period, please note the
time period.

NAME AND TITLE _____

LIBRARY/INSTITUTION

_____ PHONE (_____) _____

1) Number of full-time equivalent (FTE) students _____

    153 responses: Range 560 – 6,695; Mean 1,766; Median 1,561

2) Total size of your library's collection _____ titles

    **108 responses: Range 39,503 – 760,000; Mean 147,405; Median
    123,535**

                                            _____ volumes

    **146 responses: Range 42,530 – 1,005,320; Mean 219,663;
    Median 162,999**

3) a. Total size of your library's audiovisual
        collection   _____ titles

    102 responses: Range 0 – 68,144; Mean 5,347; Median 3,192

    If those respondents with no audiovisual collection are
    removed:

    95 responses: Range 60 – 68,144; Mean 5,741; Median 3,377

                                            _____ volumes

    108 responses: Range 0 – 157,721; Mean 10,611; Median 4,100

    If those respondents with no audiovisual collection are
    removed:

    **101 responses: Range 60 – 157,721; Mean 11,347; Median
    4,661**

7

b. Check materials included in your collection:

154 responses

Percentages have been rounded off to nearest whole number.

134 audiocassettes		127 phonodiscs	
86%		82%	
76 audio compact discs		28 realia	
49%		18%	
79 computer software		111 slides/slide sets	
51%		72%	
108 filmstrips		134 videocassettes	
70%		86%	
95 kits		25 video discs	
61%		16%	
97 motion picture film		____ Other (Please specify:)	
63%			

art/study prints	5	3%
filmloops	3	2%
flashcards	3	2%
games	5	3%
globes	1	<1%
maps	6	4%
models	4	3%
photos/pictures	2	1%
posters	1	<1%
reel-to-reel audiotapes	4	3%
sculpture	1	<1%
transparencies	10	6%

4) For what purposes does the library acquire audiovisual materials?

148 responses

In support of classroom instruction	143	Yes	5	No
	97%		3%	
In support of individual student use	109	Yes	39	No
	74%		26%	
In support of research	59	Yes	89	No
	40%		60%	
For library/campus staff training	77	Yes	71	No
	52%		48%	

8

For use by the general public   42 Yes   106 No
                                             28%   72%

Other (Please describe) _No responses_

If all answers are NO, is there a separate campus unit
charged with these responsibilities? Please describe below.

Academic computing	1
Academic departments	3
Art department	1
Audiovisual center to manage equipment	9
Audiovisual center to manage collections	9
Audiovisual center for rental and duplicating	1
College archives	3
Educational curriculum center	1
Language center	1

5) Does your library have a separate staff for managing
audiovisual materials?

148 responses   69 Yes   79 No
                                             47%   53%

If YES, is this staff involved in:

69 responses

Selection	56	Yes	13	No
	81%		9%	
Acquisitions	48	Yes	21	No
	70%		30%	
Budget management	51	Yes	18	No
	74%		26%	
Public service	69	Yes	0	No
	100%			

6) Size of your library's total acquisition budget _____

**136 responses: Range $36,680 - $1,222,000; Mean $210,370;
Median $146,000**

7) Does your library have a separate fund or funds set aside for
acquiring audiovisual materials?

148 responses   89 Yes   59 No
                                             60%   40%

If NO, how are such materials paid for?   Please describe
below.

8) Size of your library's acquisition budget for audiovisual
    materials _____

    **86 responses: Range $100 - $55,584; Mean $10,903; Median
    $6,000**

    If there is no separate audiovisual acquisition budget,
    please estimate total annual expenditures for these
    materials. _____

    **66 responses: Range $0 - $20,000; Mean $3,469; Median
    $1,250**

    If those respondents with no audiovisual collection are
    removed:

    **46 responses: Range $100 - $20,000; Mean $4,978; Median
    $2,750**

9) Does your library use any other funds or sources of support
    for the acquisition of audiovisual materials?

    148 responses   66 Yes   82 No
                                                45%   55%
    If YES, please describe below.

    Academic departments   15   10%
    Book funds   9   6%
    Booksale receipts   1   1%
    Dean's office   2   1%
    Donations/Gifts   25   17%
    Fine money   1   1%
    Grants   23   16%
    Student fees   1   1%
    Year-end money   2   1%

10) Does your library engage in any of the following practices:

    148 responses

    Lease audiovisual materials   39 Yes   109 No
                                             26%   74%

    Purchase site or blanket licenses   46 Yes   102 No
                                             31%   69%

10

```
Videotape off-air or off-satellite        77  Yes   71  No
                                          52%        48%

Enter into other similar agreements       30  Yes  118  No
                                          20%        80%
```

If YES to any of the above, please describe below and enclose documents.

```
Film/video rental              15    10%
Purchase duplication rights     1     1%
Participate in consortium       4     3%
```

11) Does your library have a separate written collection development policy for audiovisual materials?

148 responses   11 Yes 134 No
                                           7%   93%

If YES, please describe below and enclose documents.

12) Does your library have a separate written selection policy for audiovisual materials?

148 responses   12 Yes 136 No
                                           8%   92%

If YES, please describe below and enclose documents.

13) Does your library have a separate written weeding policy for audiovisual materials?

148 responses   4 Yes 144 No
                                           3%   97%

If YES, please describe below and enclose documents.

14) Does your library have special circulation policies or limitations on the circulation of audiovisual materials?

148 responses   123 Yes   25 No
                                          83%   17%

If YES, please describe below and enclose documents.

15) Does your library operate an audiovisual reserve service for either your own materials or materials owned by departments and instructors?

153 responses   <u>93</u> Yes <u>60</u> No
                             60%   40%

If YES, please describe below and enclose documents.

16) Does your library charge any user fees for audiovisual collections or services?

153 responses   <u>30</u> Yes <u>123</u> No
                             19%   81%

If YES, please describe below and enclose documents.

Color laser copying	1
Computer paper ($.05 per sheet)	1
Non-student use of computers	1
Production services (consumable materials)	7
Refundable deposit paid by non-affiliated users:	
Per item	1
Annually	1
Rental fee ($1.00) for feature films on video for	
non-classroom use or preview	1
Rental fee for audiovisual materials	1
Tape duplication	1
Use of equipment by non-university groups	9
Use of equipment for non-instructional purposes	1

NAME AND TITLE _____

INSTITUTION _____

1. Does your library collect audiovisual materials?

    52 responses/109 questionnaires sent (48% response rate)

    _40_   Yes   If YES, please go to question #3 and complete
    77%   the rest of the questionnaire.

    _12_   No   If NO, please go to question #2.
    23%

2. Does another unit on campus collect audiovisual materials?

    12 responses

    _12_   Yes   Name of unit: _____
    100%

    _0_   No   This college does not collect audiovisual
                  materials.

    Thank you for completing this questionnaire. Please turn to
    to last page for a return address.

3. In addition to the library, does any other unit on campus
    collect audiovisual materials?

    40 responses

    _27_   Yes   Name of unit: _____
    68%

    _13_   No   The library is the only unit of this college that
    32%   collects audiovisual materials.

4. Does your library have a separate written collection
    development policy for audiovisual materials?

    40 responses

    _2_   Yes   _38_   No
    5%   95%

13

5. Does your library have a separate written selection policy for audiovisual materials?

   40 responses

   __1__ Yes   __39__ No
    3%   97%

6. Does your library have a separate written weeding policy for audiovisual materials?

   40 responses

   __0__ Yes   __40__ No
                    100%

7. Does your library have special circulation policies or limitations on the circulation of audiovisual materials?

   40 responses

   __35__ Yes   __5__ No
    88%   12%

8. Does your library operate an audiovisual reserve service for either your own materials or materials owned by departments and instructors?

   40 responses

   __34__ Yes   __6__ No
    85%   15%

INDEX TO DOCUMENTS

15

BUCKNELL UNIVERSITY

GUIDELINES FOR REQUESTING MEDIA SERVICES

- Always plan as far ahead as possible.

- Requests for **rental material** must be made in writing, and must be made at least four weeks in advance.

- Requests for **equipment operators** must be made in writing, and must be made at least two weeks in advance.

- Requests for **photographic services** must allow two to ten working days to allow adequate turn-around time to complete the work.

- Request for **equipment delivery** must be made at least one day in advance.

- All equipment is loaned on a first-come, first-served basis. Advance reservations are recommended.

FOR ADDITIONAL INFORMATION

General Media Services   524-1109
Photographic Services   524-3709

Ann de Klerk, Director of Library and Media Services
Christopher Reynolds, Coordinator of Media Services
Debra Cook-Balducci, Photographer
Richard Pauling, Technician
Thomas Carl, Technical Assistant
Marcy Hoey, Office Manager

C. Reynolds
11/89

Guide to Media Services

Ellen Clarke Bertrand Library
Bucknell University
Lewisburg, PA 17837

REGULAR OFFICE HOURS

Monday -- Friday   8:00 a.m. -- 4:00 p.m.
Hours vary during January and summer sessions. Detailed schedules are available by calling 524-1109. For after hours emergencies, call 523-1271.

OFFICE LOCATION
Roberts Hall -- Lower Level

Nymphaea scutifolia (water lily). From *Victorian Floral Illustrations: 344 Wood Engravings of Exotic Flowers and Plants.*

Offset printed mauve on lavender.

19

FACILITIES

Media Services facilities include:
- film and video viewing areas to accommodate up to 25 people
- areas for the production of basic audiovisual materials such as slides, overhead projection transparencies, audio and videotapes
- additional viewing areas located in the Bertrand Library

PRODUCTION SERVICES

Photography: a variety of photographic services, both color and black & white, are available. Professional quality prints or slides may be produced for instruction, research, publication, or display.

Video Recording and Editing: special programs, projects, activities, demonstrations, or lectures may be videotaped and retained for future use. Off-the-air videotaping and cross-format video dubbing services are also available. Both of these services are provided only to the extent allowed by copyright law. Recording guidelines may be obtained from the Media Services Office.

Overhead Transparencies: original material, photos, slides, or masters which have been prepared by hand, printed by computer, or typed, can be made into transparencies. Transparency production equipment includes a microcomputer with a plotter to create charts and graphs from computer data.

Mounting and Laminating: visual materials may be mounted or laminated to enhance their appearance for display and to preserve and protect them. Users who know these processes may use the equipment to prepare their own materials.

AUDIO VISUAL EQUIPMENT

A variety of AV equipment is available:
- video projection systems
- projectors (35mm, 16mm, 8mm, overhead, opaque, and filmstrip)
- still cameras (35mm and Polaroid)
- video recording systems
- audio-cassette recorder/players
- videodisc players
- videocassette recorder/players (VHS, Beta, 3/4 U-matic, and 8mm)
- computer LCD projection system

SATELLITE TVRO

Programs transmitted via domestic and selected international satellites may be viewed at several sites or recorded for subsequent classroom playback. Participation in national teleconferences is also possible.

PURCHASE AND RENTAL OF INSTRUCTIONAL MEDIA

Media Services staff will assist users in locating and obtaining films, videotapes, and other instructional materials from off campus sources for classroom use.

CHARGES

Users are charged for production, delivery, set up, and operator services. Equipment may be rented for personal/non-classroom use. Fee schedules are available from the Media Services Office.

TECHNICAL ASSISTANCE

Media Services will:
- provide equipment operators
- deliver and set up specialized equipment
- service and repair equipment
- provide consultation on equipment selection and installation
- produce audio visual materials

TELECONFERENCES

The TVRO viewing sites, with telephone hookups, may be used for participation in teleconferences. Plans for teleconferences should be made at least four weeks ahead of time so that all conference materials may be obtained and arrangements made to handle fees and technical details. Media Services staff will assist you in planning for teleconferences.

BERTRAND LIBRARY, LEVEL TWO

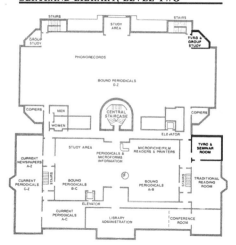

Ann de Klerk, Director of
Library and Media Services
Christopher Reynolds, Media
Services Coordinator
Roberts Hall, Lower Level
524-1109

C. Reynolds
10/89

Guide to TVRO Services

Ellen Clarke Bertrand Library
Bucknell University
Lewisburg, PA 17837

TVRO (Television Reception Only) systems are used to receive programs transmitted via communication satellites. Broadcasts from the United States, Canada, Mexico, the USSR, and some Western European countries can be received.

Natural History: Flowers and Plants. From 1800 WOODCUTS by Thomas Bewick and His School.

Offset printed mauve on tan.

TVRO SYSTEM

The TVRO satellite reception dishes, located on the Bucknell University Campus, are used for research, classroom instruction, personal enrichment, extra-curricular activities, and professional development.

TRAINING & INTRODUCTION TO TVRO

Faculty who want to use, or who would like to encourage their students to view TVRO programs may request classroom instruction on how to use the TVRO system. Individual instruction is also available.

VIEWING LOCATIONS

Bertrand Library is equipped with viewing and recording equipment. These locations are available during library hours. (See the map on the back of this brochure.) Assistance with tuning and recording is available from Library/Media Services staff.

ROOM	CAPACITY	AVAILABILITY
TVRO/Group Study	10	walk-in
TVRO/Seminar Room	30	reservation only

Other campus locations are available by reservation only and subject to availability. Equipment must be set up to permit viewing at each of these locations. Media Services staff will assist with tuning and recording.

BUILDING	ROOM	CAPACITY
Coleman Hall	101B	92
Coleman Hall	102A	128
Coleman Hall	103B	70
Vaughan Lit	205	25
Vaughan Lit.	219	18
Vaughan Lit.	Auditorium	450

HOW TO RESERVE A VIEWING LOCATION

Requests should be submitted on a TVRO Request Form to Media Services (Roberts Hall) at least 48 hours in advance of the scheduled program time. Forms are available at the Bertrand Library Reserves Desk or at Media Services.

PROGRAM SCHEDULES

Programs, broadcast times, and channels can be identified by consulting issues of Satellite Orbit or Satellite TV Weekly. Current issues are located at the Bertrand Library Reserves Desk. Subscription program services and channels dedicated to special use are encrypted (scrambled) and cannot be viewed or recorded on the Library TVRO system.

VIDEOTAPING SERVICES

When it is not possible to view programs during the scheduled transmission times, programs may be videotaped for playback at more appropriate times. All videotaping must be done in accordance with pertinent legal requirements. A tape may be retained for a limited time period, unless an off-satellite taping license has been obtained from the program distributor. Detailed copyright guidelines are available upon request from Media Services.

HOW TO REQUEST A VIDEOTAPING

Requests should be submitted on a TVRO Request Form to Media Services (Roberts Hall) at least 48 hours in advance of the scheduled program time. Forms are available at the Bertrand Library Reserves Desk or at Media Services.

COLLEGE OF WOOSTER

I

A GUIDE TO AUDIO-VISUAL SERVICES

Photoduplicated, with canary yellow
covers. Sections are tabbed. 25

The primary charge of Audio-Visual Services at the College of Wooster is to support the academic program of the College. As such, we make available various sorts of equipment and production services to students, faculty, and staff. Pending the availability of staff and equipment, such services are provided to non-College users, as well. We divide our categories of service to these various user groups in the following way:

Academic

Equipment fees are waived and delivery services are provided for regularly taught courses that are listed in the academic catalogue. Such users are not charged for production costs, but rather only for materials, such as blank tape.

Non-Academic/College Related

Equipment fees are waived for the college related activities of groups or individuals on campus that are not directly a part of a regularly taught course. Delivery services are not provided for such activities. Examples of *Non-Academic/College Related users* include, but are not restricted to: the Student Activities Board; clubs; and sections. Such users are charged for the cost of productions and the materials associated with those productions.

Please Note: Due to the limited availability of items as video players and cameras, we may not always be able to provide you with such equipment. We will be happy to provide you with local sources in Wooster where such equipment can be rented.

Non-College Related

A non-College of Wooster user shall be defined as an individual or group that is not part of a regular academic or administrative activity at the College. Examples of *Non-College users* include, but are not restricted to: summer sports camps; other schools, including elementary, secondary, and post-secondary institutions; local businesses; local civic groups; and, local community members. Equipment rental fees are charged (see **RATES FOR SERVICES & EQUIPMENT**). Delivery not provided.

CATEGORIES OF SERVICE • WHO, WHAT, WHERE

Each year the Audio-Visual Department receives requests for approximately 800 films, videotapes and the related equipment. In order to accommodate these requests and to comply with the policies of the film distributors **and** of our department, please follow the procedures listed below:

1. Requests for films and videotapes must be written on an A.V. film order form 8 weeks in advance of the showdate. We can process an order in 3 to 5 days. The distributors need 4 to 6 weeks to process our order. The titles owned by the College Library must also be in writing, on an A.V. form and ordered at least one week in advance. Phone orders <u>will</u> <u>not</u> be accepted.

2. When completing the A.V. Film Order Form, please fill in all of the blanks as indicated on the form. Film and video reference catalogs are available in the A.V. study area. List an alternate date, at least 7 days before or after the original date. The chairperson of your department <u>must</u> sign this form. Orders cannot be processed without this signature.

3. The film distributors ask that we follow specific rules in regard to scheduled dates:
   a. do not reschedule a showdate if the order has been confirmed.
   b. the film/video must be returned via United Parcel Services the morning after the confirmed showdate. If rented materials are not returned on time, distributors generally charge us a late fee, possibly hurting our credibility with the company. Customer pick-up **means** customer return. Please return the films/videos before 10:00 am so that we can process them and send them back in the UPS shipment.

Equipment In the Classroom

• *16mm films* - An order for a 16mm film is an automatic order for the projector and screen. One of our students will deliver the film and the necessary equipment the evening before the showdate. They will thread the film and check that the equipment is working properly. After your class screening please leave the film with the projector, in the classroom, and we will pick it up later in the day.

• *1/2" VHS video* - Special arrangements must be made through Tony Bordac for the use of this type of equipment. As with films, the videotape is ordered through Patti McVay.

For further information on the general availability of A.V. equipment, refer to the section on **EQUIPMENT SERVICES**.

FILM & VIDEO SERVICES

We have a wide variety of equipment available for you to use, as you can see by the list that follows. While staffing limitations prevent us from providing personnel to run this equipment for you, we are more than willing to give you or a designated student personalized instruction in the use of any machine we have. *We will deliver equipment for any classroom-related activities if given 24-hour notice. If notice is given in less than 24 hours, patron will have to pick-up equipment in A-V.* See **FILM & VIDEO SERVICES** for information on how to rent or purchase such media for classroom use.

Audio

Our equipment pool includes:

• *Cassette Recorder/Players* - a good assortment of very portable machines that you can use for playback of teaching materials in a classroom or for reviewing notes at home. The recording capability of most of our cassette machines is marginal, but adequate for transcription purposes if you keep a machine's built-in microphone fairly close to the speaker. Higher quality recorders for special interviews are also available.

• *Phonograph Players* - for playing records in class.

Film

Our equipment pool includes:

• *16mm Movie Projectors* - these easy-threading machines can be delivered to an instructor's classroom along with the film, or classes can come to our Film Preview Room (Level One of the Library) where we keep two projectors permanently stationed.

• *35mm Slide Projectors* - we maintain a good stock of Kodak carousel projectors. Faculty can check them out for up to a year at a time.

• *Overhead Transparency Projectors* - These "electric chalkboards" can be checked out to faculty --- first come, first served --- on a yearly basis, too. We also have the facilities to produce professional-quality overhead transparencies for you (see **PRODUCTION SERVICES**).

• *Opaque Projectors* - These bulky, but useful machines are popular with Art and Theater students for the purpose of enlarging drawings and designs.

Video

The majority of our video equipment is dedicated to the 1/2" VHS format. We offer 3/4" tape playback from our central office. We do not have equipment compatible with the Beta format. Available equipment and facilities include:

•*Film Preview Room* - located on Level One of Andrews Library, this facility seats about 40 people.

•*Video Projection System* - located in the 230-seat Mateer auditorium, this system is ideal for large group viewing. The system features sophisticated digital visual effects and high fidelity sound. Use of this room is scheduled through the Facilities Office in Lowry Center.

•*WoosterNet Video Network* - we can send video programs from the A-V department to classrooms equipped with taps into the WoosterNet computer network. This includes most rooms in Scovel, Taylor, and Scheide Music Center. In Kauke, WoosterNet is currently available in rooms 2, 26, 200, 201, 202, and 229.

•*Portable Video Players* - these easy-to-use players can be checked out of the A-V department and used in classrooms already equipped with video monitors. Most of the academic buildings have at least one portable video monitor on a cart that we move between classrooms. In a few cases, such as Lean Lecture Hall, the physical layout of the room prevents us from providing video service at this time. Check with our office for details.

NOTE: Due to limited resources, we may not always be able to provide Non-Academic users with video players or cameras. In such cases we can refer you to local sources of such equipment in the city of Wooster. Just ask at the Service Counter.

LIFE IN THE FAST LANE ---- A word of warning----
Most VHS machines are able to record a tape at three different speeds:

SP for 2-hours of programming
LP for 4-hours   SLP for 6-hours

Our portable video players are meant to play tapes that were recorded at **SP**, the 2-hour speed that is used by commercial tape producers. A tape recorded at home on either **LP** or **SLP** speed will show up too fast on your TV set when you play it on our machine. Your other option in this case would be to schedule time in the Film Preview Room, which is equipped with a multi-speed machine.

EQUIPMENT SERVICES

Not only do we provide equipment for you, but we can help you produce materials to use on that equipment. Our production services can be broken down into three categories: the creation and duplication of audio and video tapes; the creation of color and black & white slides and prints; various graphics services. For associated service charges, see **RATES FOR SERVICES AND MATERIALS.**

Tape Production

Please Note: We will not duplicate copyrighted materials unless you can furnish written proof that you have secured duplication rights for the tape(s) in question.

•*Real-time Duplication of Audio Tape (cassette and open-reel)* --- A "real-time" copy is simply one where a master tape is played on one machine at normal speed, while another machine records it. The length of this process takes as long as the original master takes to play. We charge for this service by the hour.

•*High-Speed Duplication of Audio Tape (cassette only)* --- Those who want to save money and do not need the high quality reproduction provided by real-time duplication will probably be quite satisfied with high-speed copying. This less costly process can produce a copy of a 90-minute cassette in several minutes. This method is ideal for duplicating speeches and non-critical musical recordings. Audiophiles generally do not like this process because it tends to lose the very high and low frequencies of a dynamic musical performance, although many people are quite satisfied by the quality of high-speed musical recordings. We have a "per tape" charge for this service.

•*"Normal" vs "Chrome" Tape* --- You have the choice of two different types of tape when you turn in an audio production request. If you want us to copy a speech or a non-critical musical event, you will probably be satisfied with a *normal bias* tape. However, if you want to preserve the fine tonal details of a musical performance, you will probably find a *high bias* or *chrome* tape more to your liking. The chromium alloy formulation on high bias tapes is more sensitive to a wider range of frequencies.

•*Videotaping Services* --- Our video crew, utilizing industrial-grade VHS equipment, is available to tape anything from a foreign langauge skit to a major lecture on campus. This service is available free of charge (less materials) for all academic projects, **pending** the availability of staff and equipment. All others will be charged an hourly production fee, plus materials. Post-production editing is available for a further production fee. Given the high demand and our limited resources for this service, requests will be considered on a case-by-case basis.

•*Real-time Video Duplication*--- We will copy your VHS master tape for you, at our regular rates, as long as you own or have secured the duplication rights for the tape. High speed video duplication is not available.

We also have the facilities to offer optical transfers of master tapes recorded outside of the U.S. on either the PAL or SECAM standards. This process involves nothing more than aiming a video camera at a multi-standard television monitor. The result, while not the quality of a more expensive professional transfer, still offers the patron the ability to obtain a viewable tape that can be played on U.S. equipment.

Photographic Production

•We have the facilities to produce color slides or black & white prints from your original artwork, or from books or magazines. We can also duplicate slides. As with our various taping services, we reserve the right to refuse such service if your request violates applicable copyright regulations.

Graphics Production

We offer a variety of graphics services, including:

•*Overhead Transparencies* - using your masters, we can produce transparencies that can be used in class on overhead projectors. Anything that can be photocopied can be turned into an overhead transparency.

•*Dry-Mounting* - we can take an illustration provided by you and glue it to a stiff piece of cardboard for preservation purposes. Unlike using *Elmer's*, our process will give you perfectly flat adhesion.

•*Laminating* - another preservation service we offer is to cover your flat original with a protective plastic coating.

•*Cloth-Backing* - if you want to make an original map or diagram stronger, but do not want to laminate it with plastic, you might consider this process, which applies a reinforcing cloth material to the back of your illustration.

•*Kroy Lettering* - this process is ideal for creating printed labels on a strip of clear plastic tape. A variety of type fonts are available.

PRODUCTION SERVICES

Cost Justification

Materials Costs

These prices are calculated from a formula that takes into consideration the base cost of the materials, plus shipping and processing charges. In many cases our prices are higher than those at local discount stores because we are not in business to sell blank tapes and so forth (materials for classroom-related requests are sold at lower prices). By the same token, we do not discourage patrons from purchasing their materials, such as tapes, from other sources as long as those materials are made by reputable name-brand manufacturers, such as TDK, Maxell, Sony, and Fuji. *We reserve the right to refuse to complete production requests accompanied by what we deem to be inferior materials (e.g. --- audiocassette tapes that are sold in bags of three for $1.00; videocassette tapes with hyped-up "brand names" such as "Laser" or "High Quality.")*

Equipment and Production Costs

These prices are calculated from a formula that takes into consideration such things as the original cost of the equipment, the estimated useful life of the equipment, and the replacement of such expendable items as projection lamps.

ᄆᄇᄆ

AUDIO PRODUCTION

IN-HOUSE PRODUCTION
Real-time duplication, between like or different formats $5.00/hr* (minimum)

High-speed duplication. Cassette-to-cassette only. $1.50/ea*

* Plus cost of tapes

32

RATES FOR SERVICES & MATERIALS

AUDIO TAPE COST:

TDK D-60 (normal bias) $2.00
For *regular quality* audio reproduction

TDK D-90 (normal bias) $2.75
For *regular quality* audio reproduction

TDK SA-90 (high bias/chrome) $3.25
For *high quality* music reproduction

Tape stock is not rented or loaned. All rates subject to change.

ᴠᴀᴠ

VIDEO PRODUCTION

REMOTE PRODUCTION $5.00/hr*
Color, single camera, 1/2 " VTR, videographer, basic lighting and audio.
Includes set-up/take-down time.

IN-HOUSE PRODUCTION
Real-time duplication $5.00/tape* (minimum)
(3/4-inch & VHS only)

Editing (VHS only) $5.00/hr*

VIDEO TAPE COST:

Maxell T-120 HGX (high grade) $8.00

NOTE: All videotaping requests must be made at least 10 days in advance. Hourly rates are quoted less videotape charges. Tape stock is not rented or loaned. All rates subject to change.

* Plus cost of tape

33

PHOTOGRAPHIC PRODUCTION

Slide production includes film/processing charges. There is a 15 slide minimum on each order.

Slide creation from your original art (includes color film)	$1.00/ea
Slide-to-slide copies	$1.00/ea
Black & White prints (8x10) made from original art. 3 photo minimum on each order	$3.00/ea

ᴚᴒ

GRAPHICS PRODUCTION

Transparency film (Thermofax method)	.35/ea
Write-on transparency	.15/ea
Transparency Frames	.25/ea
Roll Lamination (24" maximum width)	.35/running ft
Seal Press Lamination Film	.35/piece
Dry-mounting tissue	.30/running ft
Dry-backing cloth	3.75/running ft
Kroy lettering	.50/ft
Service Charge (if we do the work)	Materials cost x 2

EQUIPMENT RENTAL
(8.00a.m.-4.00p.m.)

	Per day
PROJECTORS	
16mm motion picture (sound)	15.00
2x2 slide-carousel (includes tray, remote)	10.00
Sound/Slide synchronized projector (Caramate)	10.00
35mm filmstrip	3.00
Opaque	5.00
Overhead	5.00
8mm silent	5.00
MISCELLANEOUS VISUAL EQUIPMENT	
Screen, standard tripod	5.00
Projection stand or cart	3.00
Dissolve unit	5.00
AUDIO	
Tape recorder (cassette or reel-to-reel)	5.00
Record player	5.00
Microphone (standard, w/stand)	5.00

Audio recording set-up (incl/microphone, stands, mixer, recorder, cables and adaptors)   15.00

Sync cassette recorder (Caramate)   10.00

VIDEO

Portable 1/2" VHS Video Player   15.00

19" color monitor   15.00

EASTERN OREGON STATE COLLEGE

Educational Media Center • Eastern Oregon State College

Services Provided

The Educational Media Center's three operating units (Multi-media Collection, Production, and the Audiovisual Equipment System) function within three categories: Instructional Support, Instructional Development, and Non-Instructional Services.

I. Instructional Support

Generally, this category contains all services which are associated with the direct support of instruction by the distribution and utilization of audiovisual equipment and materials on campus.

A. *AV Equipment Distribution System*

Drawing upon a central equipment inventory in the Educational Media Center (EMC), as well as equipment pools in separate instructional buildings, EMC staff accept reservations, schedule, deliver, and pick up AV equipment used by faculty to support instruction. Faculty, staff and students may also pick up and return equipment to the Center.

B. *AV Equipment Repair and Maintenance*

An EMC technician monitors equipment use rates and the general condition of equipment in use around campus. When a piece of equipment fails:
..... it is determined if it is repairable
..... if not, it is taken out of operation
..... if repairable by the technician, it is repaired and returned to service
..... if not, it is sent to a commercial repair facility.

C. *Software Library* (films, filmstrips, slides, slide-tape shows, records, videotapes)

EMC's library of instructional software is for the most part acquired by academic departments on campus, and is then stored in the Center to facilitate distribution. All materials housed in the EMC are thoroughly cataloged. Software may be:
- checked out by students, faculty and staff,
- checked out by town patrons according to availability,
- duplicated as permitted by copyright laws utilizing the Center's tape duplication facilities.

D. *Film/Video Rental Services*

EMC maintains a number of services related to the rental of instructional films and videotapes for faculty. These include:
..... maintaining an up-to-date library of Instructional Film (and other) catalogs,
..... placing orders for faculty members, informing them of completed booking arrangements and reserving equipment,
..... delivering, setting up, and frequently showing films/videos upon arrival,
..... returning films after use.

E. *Instruction in Media Operation*

EMC staff train various college clients in the use of instructional media, including:
..... professors, so that they might provide media support for their classes,
..... pre-service teachers, to prepare them for the proper utilization of instructional media in both student teaching and when they are employed full time,
..... other students, so that they may utilize learning carrels for independent study.

F. Instructional Software Preview Services
EMC will contact vendors on behalf of faculty members to secure instructional software (films, videotapes, slide-tape shows, etc.) for preview.

G. Other Resources
EMC offers a variety of instructional materials to students, faculty members, and the college service population. Items sold include: film, audio cassettes, video cassettes, mounting tissue, laminate, etc. **All items are sold at cost.**

II. Instructional Development
This category includes all those activities which result in the creation of new materials and/or the alteration of instructional delivery systems for the improvement of teaching and learning at Eastern Oregon State College.

A. Consultative Services
Any faculty member wishing to design, produce and implement changes in the manner in which he or she delivers instruction is invited to consult with the EMC coordinator for assistance with:
1. ... identifying project objectives
2. ... selecting appropriate strategies for achieving objectives
3. ... designing relevant materials, etc.
4. ... implementing instructional alternatives

B. Graphics and Photographics Services
EMC current services in this area support such activities as slide-tape program development, posters, fliers, signs, notices, etc. Specific services include:
1. Black & white development and printing (EX: providing College Relations support by developing and printing their photographic requests)
2. Color slide development and mounting
3. Slide duplication
4. Computer-graphic page layout utilizing a large database of programs and images
5. Newsletter production
6. Lamination of materials
7. Dry-mounting
8. Overhead Transparencies

C. Audio Production Services
EMC assists students and faculty in the production and utilization of audio-based instructional materials in several ways. Foreign language students use audio cassettes prepared by the EMC. High Speed duplication equipment makes "dupes" available for only the cost of the tape.

III. Non-Instructional Services
This category includes services which are available to other state agencies, non-profit organizations and the community at large. Examples:

A. Equipment delivery, set-up and pick-up for off-campus groups who meet on campus, according to an established fee schedule.

B. Check-out of EMC multi-media materials and equipment according to availability. Equipment check-out follows an established fee schedule.

6/11/90

Educational Media Center
Materials Checkout Policy:

Faculty* & Ad. Staff: All materials - 2 weeks

                                 *End of quarter by arrangement

Students*:   All materials (except videotapes) - 2 weeks

                                 Videotapes - Overnight or over weekend

                                 * Student I.D. required

Town Patrons*:   All materials (except videotapes) - 2 weeks

                                 Videotapes - Overnight or over weekend

                                 * Town Patron card required (available free from Library)

Note: All materials (excluding those checked out quarterly) are renewable by telephone. Materials checked out quarterly must be returned to the EMC for inventory purposes and/or be checked by a member of the EMC staff, prior to renewal.

Items which cannot be located will be considered lost and the borrower will be charged for them.

All materials are available for check-out, with the following exceptions:

Reserve materials: No out-of-building checkout unless otherwise noted.

Records: **General Collection:** Out of building checkout to Eastern music faculty only. **Holmes Collection:** No out of building checkout. See EMC policy book for additional information under "Record Collection Policy".

Videotapes: No out-of-building checkout of "French In Action" videotapes without permission from Dr. Spronk, ext 1599.

No out-of-building checkout of the following tapes without permission from Prof. Gary Feasel, ext 1367 or 1361 (PE office):

    "Red Cross Standard First Aid", "American Red Cross Community CPR", "Spinal Injury Management", "Infant & Preschool Aquatic Program", & "Longfellow's Whale Tales".

Individual slides: No out-of-building checkout of the Frederick Hartt Art History slides without permission from Prof. Judd Koehn, ext 1584, or Dr. Shahbazi, ext 1709.

(3)

Educational Media Center

Circulation of EMC Materials Policy

Fine Schedule

General Circulation -- Multimedia materials:

.25 per day

No charge is made for the first 3 days an item is overdue but a charge of $1.00 will be assessed on the 4th day, plus .25 per day thereafter. The maximum fine is $10.00 per item. Upon reaching the $10.00 amount, a $6.00 replacement charge will be automatically assessed against you. Flagrant rule violation could result in a fine of $1.00 per day.

Reserve Materials:

Hourly Materials: .25 per hour
Daily Materials: $1.00 per day
Maximum Fine of $10.00 per item. Flagrant rule violation could result in a fine of $1.00 per hour.

Other Charges:

Failure to promptly return materials recalled by the Educational Media Center: $1.00 per day.

Lost Materials: The borrower will be charged the replacement cost of any lost item, plus the amount of the fine incurred prior to the item being reported missing, plus a service charge of $6.00 per item.

Damaged or Mutilated Materials: A charge for repair or replacement to be determined by the Educational Media Center.

The above fines and charges comply with the regulations for fines and charges established by the Oregon State System of Higher Education.

8/24/89

(4)

Educational Media Center

Record Collection Policy

General Collection

Out of building checkout to Eastern Oregon State College music faculty only.

Records may be listened to in the EMC, or circulating copies on audiocassette will be made at patron request by EMC staff as quickly as possible (no charge).

Circulating audiocassettes will be labeled accordingly and shelved separately.

Records will be placed on reserve as requested.

John E. Holmes Memorial Collection

No out of building checkout.

Records may be listened to in the EMC, or circulating copies on audiocassette will be made at patron request by EMC staff as quickly as possible (no charge).

Circulating audiocassettes will be labeled accordingly and shelved separately.

Records are housed on open shelves in the EMC, near the general record collection, with a detection system tape in each item.

Each jacket is stamped "John E. Holmes Memorial Collection" and is numbered.

The index file that was donated with the records is nearby and will be used until an integrated computer system is established, at which time the collection will be fully cataloged.

There is a separate list of Compact Disk titles posted.

When there is a request for placing records on reserve for student use, a cassette tape copy will be made and used.

Computer graphic produced signs identify the collection.

1/29/90

(5)

43

Educational Media Center

Film / Video Rental Policy

The EMC provides faculty / staff service for rental of films and videotapes for educational purposes. A large collection of University and other rental catalogs is housed in the EMC. Faculty / staff are welcome to look at these catalogs when they have need of rental films and/or videotapes and do not have specific titles in mind.

To maximize service and minimize telephone charges, all film / video rental orders must be received at least two months ahead of the desired show date to allow for booking by mail. (Rental fees and telephone charges for requests that necessitate booking by telephone will be billed back to the appropriate school or department).

Rental requests may be submitted in person, by mail or telephone. Please list titles, show date(s), alternate dates if desired, and source, if known.

EMC film / video booking personnel will notify the individual who placed the request when a rental is confirmed. EMC recommends scheduling equipment and requesting an operator, if desired, well ahead of the show date.

8/24/89

(15)

Educational Media Center

Gift Policy

The EMC welcomes gifts or donations of multimedia materials. Such materials, whether solicited or unsolicited, are checked carefully against existing collections and added to them if deemed appropriate. The EMC reserves the right in all cases to determine appropriateness and disposition of donated materials. Duplicate or inappropriate titles are offered to other Media Centers, donated to such charitable efforts as the AAUW Book Fair, or made available to the campus community through materials sales.

The EMC cannnot act as appraiser. Upon acceptance of materials, the Coordinator of EMC will acknowledge the gift in writing.

Lack of separate space ordinarily prevents the EMC from preserving donated collections as intact separate entities. These are in most cases incorporated into existing general or special collections.

Gift items will be memorialized with a special label provided by the EMC, at the request of the donor.

8/24/89

(16)

EVANGEL COLLEGE

EVANGEL COLLEGE MEDIA CENTER HANDBOOK

This handbook contains the general policies under which the library media center operates. The center exists to serve the media needs of the Evangel Community. The shared needs of a community such as Evangel College are often complex and don't lend themselves to absolute laws, but rather guidelines that help insure sharing the resources fairly. The staff of the library understands that exceptions are likely when meeting community needs with media equipment and software.

The Library Director and the entire library staff will assist in serving the community. Routine requests may be made of any library staff member. Questions and exceptional needs should be directed to the Media Coordinator at Ext. 245 or Library Director at Ext. 268. The Library Committee serves in an advisory capacity to the library/media center staff.

MEDIA BUDGET

Departmental budgets for the media requests will be available from the Academic Dean's office. The budgets will be administered by the Library Director according to quideline agreed to in Academic Council.

PURCHASING

All purchase order requests will originate in the library. Ordering of materials will be done by the library staff and materials will be received in the library. Media request forms will be provided to the departments. Budget accounting will be provided to insure proper distribution of funds. Software acquisitions will be for adopted formats to help standardize equipment in the center. Computer formats are IBM PC-DOS and Apple DOS and the VCR format is VHS.

Only computer software designed to run specific programs of an educational nature will be purchased with library media funds. Applications software must be purchased with other funds. Usually computer software will be copied and the original disk stored in a safe in the library and the copy, with the documentation, sent to the department.

Equipment purchases will be through the normal capital outlay process from requests made by the library staff. Suggestions for equipment purchases should be submitted to the library director before capital outlay is divided each fall.

LOCATION AND STORAGE

The library staff will be charged with the responsibility of maintaining and storing all media equipment and software purchased with college funds or funds donated for media purchase. If donor conditions dictate storing the equipment or software in a specific location, those conditions will be honored during the regular college term. Donated equipment or software may be temporarily used in other areas to meet special, emergency, or exceptional needs of the college. These exceptions will be discussed with departmental or agencies heads, if he or she is available, before the equipment is used.

1

All media equipment will remain accessible to the library staff during school hours and vacations for inspection, maintenance, and use elsewhere. Off campus use of donated equipment and software will follow the same guidelines as those for other media software and equipment unless the college accepts other conditions from donors. All equipment will be stored in the media center during the summer unless other arrangements are made with the department staff for secure storage.

Equipment or software will be stored at locations on campus which will enhance the use of the equipment or software. As a general policy storage will be either in the library or in building 13. During the summer and whenever servicing is necessary, all equipment and software may be moved to a location convenient to the library staff.

DELIVERY REQUESTS EQUIPMENT AND SOFTWARE

All equipment and software delivery requests must be submitted to the library not later than 3:30 P.M. for the next school day. Requests should be submitted on forms available from the library staff. The library maintains two drop boxes for requests-one in the humanities office in building 12 and one in the Biblical studies office in building 31. Requests must be in the boxes before 3:00 P.M. to insure delivery for the next school day. Any equipment may be requested for same day use by faculty, however, delivery and set up cannot be promised. It will be the faculty member's responsibility to pick up the equipment and return it unless the media staff can arrange delivery and return.   In a legitimate emergency, such as illness, phone requests for same day delivery will be honored, if possible. Please make such requests as early as possible to insure delivery and return.

When equipment is delivered to a campus location, the delivery, care, and return of the equipment and software is the responsibility of the library staff. As good stewards of college property, staff and faculty members should take reasonable care of the equipment that they are using. This may include securing the equipment and/or software temporarily until a library staff member can return it to storage.

When a faculty or staff member borrows equipment or software from the media center for use on or off campus, it is entirely his/her responsibility to care for the equipment or software until it is properly returned and credit is given by the library staff. The faculty or staff member who does not give reasonable care to software or equipment may be found liable for repairs or replacement by the business manager or academic dean.

If media equipment is to be used at hours when the library staff is not available, such as on Saturday evening, the faulty member must make arrangements with the media staff to borrow and return the equipment at hours when the library is open. Responsibility for securing and operating the equipment will be on the faculty member who arranges for the use of the equipment. Instruction for proper use will be given when the equipment is delivered to the borrower, if requested. Users may attempt to telephone library staff at home if problems are encountered after normal library hours.

Any faculty member who discovers any unattended or abandoned equipment or software that may belong to the college should call the library so it can be secured until ownership is established. The faculty member should secure it in his/her office if the library staff cannot be contacted.

2

REPAIRS

It will be the responsibility of the media center to maintain and repair all media equipment that the college owns, except specialize equipment (such as reading machines). The library staff is charged with sending the equipment to service centers and paying out of its budget the cost for service.

No other faculty or staff member should send or take media equipment from the campus for repair. No one should attempt to service any media equipment other than emergency repairs, such as changing bulbs.

OFF CAMPUS USE

The media center exists to serve all the media needs of the staff and faculty in their college related activities. Faculty and staff members may request media equipment or software for use off campus during speaking or ministry engagements where the main emphasis is supporting the educational role or public relations of the college. Media equipment is not intended for personal or other purposes off campus by the faculty and staff. Software may be used for personal preview provided it is not scheduled for other use.

Media equipment and software are primarily intended for classroom and related educational use. Equipment may be rented for a fee for use by organized student groups who have a faculty or staff sponsor. The faculty or staff member will be responsible for the equipment and must sign the rental forms. Off campus rental will be encouraged whenever possible. If the library staff deems that an operator is required, compensation will be paid by the renter.

Media equipment may not be rented or borrowed by local churches, private or public schools, and other groups, except as noted above. Software may be loaned whenever loaning it will enhance the public relations efforts of the college.

The media center will attempt to meet the needs of faculty and staff who are hosting conferences and workshops on campus. The faculty member may need to borrow or rent off campus when requiring large amounts of equipment.

Equipment requests for classroom use by instructors will take precedence over conference and workshop requests if the classroom requests are made before the commitment of equipment is made to the conference or workshop.

CHAPEL USE

The use of media equipment in the chapel sometimes requires special treatment. There is a 16MM projector with a special lens located in the chapel for use only in that building. The media center has some special equipment for the chapel. Please give the staff one-week's notice for using media equipment in the chapel so the proper lenses can be secured and fitted.

SEMESTER USE

Requests for semester loan of equipment and software should be made with extreme discretion. If the software requested is not likely to be requested by another faculty member or if it can be returned on a one day's notice the request may be honored. Semester loan of equipment will only be considered when the equipment will be used at least twice a week by the instructor. Such requests may be honored if there is sufficient equipment available to meet the normal needs, and if the faculty members agrees that the equipment will be readily available when it is not in use.

3

OPERATORS

The media center will furnish operators for 16 MM projectors and video cameras unless the borrower has had experience with the model being used and does not wish the operator to stay. An operator will not be provided with other equipment unless requested by the user. If the user is unfamiliar with operation of the equipment, he/she should make arrangements for instruction prior to delivery of the equipment. The operator will not act as classroom monitor.

LARGE MONITORS

The media center has two 26 inch television monitors available. These are very large and heavy. These will only be delivered when requested for large groups in large rooms such as 31-1. During inclement weather, the staff may substitute smaller, less expensive equipment. Two televisions or monitors can be run from one VCR for larger groups.

VIDEO CAMERAS

The media center has two video cameras. These are intended for taping special sessions; not for routine classroom taping. Taping of smaller groups will be done at a location agreeable to both the requesting faculty and library staff, usually in the library. Unless other arrangements are made, the staff will provide operators for all taping sessions. Normally the video cameras will be used only on-campus.

RENTING EQUIPMENT

As a general policy, the library staff cannot honor requests for the rental of commercial equipment unless it has been included in the department's budget. This would include large screen televisions and computer output projectors.

The staff will assist anyone needing such equipment if it has been budgeted and if the request is made well in advance. The staff will make arrangements to have the equipment delivered, secured, and returned.

COMPUTERS

Computer equipment is not part of the media center's equipment. Arrangements for the use of computer equipment in conjunction with media equipment must be made first through the computer center and then through the media center.

FEES

The library staff will charge for some services such as video or audio tape duplication or video taping. The rates will be available from the staff. Normally only tapes purchased by the staff will be used for duplication and taping. Inferior video tapes will not be used on the media center machines.

The library staff will follow copyright guidelines in duplicating any software. The staff will not copy materials that are copyrighted unless permission is granted.

4

OFF THE AIR TAPING

The media center will honor requests for off the air taping of television programs under the copyright guidelines of fair use. (Copies are available in each department office and in the library.) Requests must be specific and indicate the classes for which the program is being taped.

Tapes will be erased after the time specified in the fair use guidelines. All tapes of programs remain the property of the library and must be stored in the media center when not in use.

The library staff cannot be responsible for failures to tape programs because of power outages or program shifting by the station. The quality of reception of some stations is poor because of a lack of antenna system in the library. In some cases, taping of programs may be available from cable stations if prior arrangements are made with the director.

CONCLUSION

The library staff will try to accommodate as many requests as possible. It is the desire of the staff to serve each member of the community and to enhance classroom teaching and to make the use of media as easy as possible. The guidelines are used to help everyone to share the scarce resources as fairly possible. Problems or suggestions should be directed to the library staff.

5

FRANKLIN AND MARSHALL COLLEGE

SECTION: **IMS**
SUBJECT: General Information

The Office of Instructional Media Services (IMS) promotes and supports the integration of non-print media into the College curriculum and the resulting classroom instruction. IMS offers the College community a wide variety of media services, most of which are anchored by the **Media Center** in Stager Hall. During the Spring and Fall Semesters, the IMS is open from:

Monday-Thursday	**8AM-10PM**
Friday	**8AM-4:30PM**
Sunday	**1PM -10PM.**

Hours during the summer and vacation periods may vary, but are primarily Monday-Friday from 8:30AM-12 Noon; 1-4:30PM. The IMS phone number is 291-4019 (on-campus x-4019). The IMS offers:
- •Non-print collection support services (storage and utilization space)
- •Video support services, including:
  - -videocassette and videodisc playback classroom delivery
  - -video duplication and off-air (TV) recording (copyright permitting)
  - -recording of a live campus event on videotape
  - -large screen computer display for classroom presentations
  - -videotape searching (for purchase or rental) in catalogs
  - -sophisticated, in-studio & on-location, instructional videotape production
- •35mm slide production service and 35mm photography
- •Audiovisual equipment loan, delivery and pick up service
- •Audiotape production services (incl: stereo transfer and studio recording)
- •Audiovisual equipment repair and maintenance service for departments
- •Audiovisual supplies for the campus
- •Audiovisual consultation service
- •Graphics services (transparencies, dry mounting and laminating)
- •Technical assistance and support for Hensel Hall and Stahr Auditorium
- •Satellite Television Reception Services (including teleconferencing)

The need for **Planning Ahead** can not be overemphasized. All equipment reservations for classroom utilization must be made at least 24 hours in advance (one week's advance notice is preferred) and there are certain physical limitations to which types of equipment can be used on certain parts of the campus. Any equipment and/or personnel reservations for events held outside of the classroom (Hensel Hall, Stahr Auditorium, evening lectures, etc) should be made at the earliest possible time. No requests to reserve Hensel Hall or Stahr Auditorium will be accommodated with less than 48 hours notice (two week's advance notice is preferred) . Any questions concerning planning for audiovisual support should be channeled to the IMS Director.

SECTION: IMS
SUBJECT: Media Center

The **Media Center**, located on the ground floor of Stager Hall, offers students and faculty an environment to utilize the College's non-print collections: presently over four thousand phonodisc recordings, two thousand audiocassettes (mostly modern language and music), four hundred compact disc recordings, eight hundred videocassettes and seventy laser videodiscs. Students have access to the materials by using one of the thirty listening/viewing carrels which are equipped with either turntables, CD players, stereo audiocassette decks, TV and VCRs, slide or 16mm film projectors.There are six carrels equipped with televisions and VHS format VCR's in the **Media Center** to view videocassettes at their leisure. This provides an excellent way to preview materials, complete remedial work, or catch up on missed assignments. Professors may also assign students to watch videocassettes in the Media Center on their own time. Videocassettes housed at the Media Center are to be used at the center; **video materials do not circulate**. Two exceptions are when cassettes are used for a presentation or class on campus and when professors sign them out (24 hour sign-out period) to prepare for a class. An individual or group can watch a pre-recorded videodisc or use the interactive video/microcomputer workstation in the Media Center. The interactive workstation combines optical videodiscs with Macintosh HyperCard software to control the video. It is also possible to watch satellite TV programs.

The **Media Center** also includes high speed cassette duplication of foreign language tapes, transfer of materials from records and open reel tapes onto cassettes, maintaining the audio cassette inventory and the operation of the twenty carrel audio cassette listening facility. The following departments have audiocassettes filed in the Media Center library: American Studies, Biology, Drama, English, French, German, Italian, Music, Portuguese, Religious Studies, Russian, Sociology., and Spanish. The Media Center now houses fifteen stereo audiocassette listening carrels, two mono audiocassette carrels, five stereo high fidelity (phonograph) stations, and three compact disc players for the students' listening. Modern language professors may also assign dictation exercises for students to complete at the Media Center.

The F&M record collection is housed in Stager Hall. High fidelity stereo turntables and compactdisc players are located there for listening purposes. **Records do not circulate.** Exception: professors may sign out records for a class or campus production. They should be returned immediately afterward.

The **Media Center** also houses various F&M 35mm slide collections and has carrel-mounted 35mm slide Caramate projectors to allow students and professors to view slides. The Media Center also has a carrel-mounted 16mm film projectors professor and students can use for previewing films in the Media Center.

In 1987, the Media Center installed a satellite television downlink. This allows the College to host teleconferences and, through it's membership in the SCOLA consortium, Franklin and Marshall now provides students with daily television news broadcasts originating from around the globe.

In 1988, the Media Center installed a limited cable network to the dormitories and the College Center, which provides the students with the Lancaster cable television service (38 channels) as well as an on-campus television channel (WFMC-TV). A Cable Television club has been formed to provide programming for WFMC-TV. To mention but a few options, this programming may include an electronic bulletin board, satellite stations, "talk-show" style interviews, playback of educational videocasettes, etc.

The IMS administers some special spaces for the campus; specifically **Stahr Auditorium** and **Hensel Hall.** Stahr Auditorium (170 seats) in Stager Hall which has a rear screen projection system for video, computer data, 16mm film and 35mm slides; as well as an electronic overhead projector for transparencies or any opaque material needed to illustrate a point. It has been designed to accommodate lectures and events of special stature, as well as regular classes which utilize the sophisticated audiovisual projection equipment. Hensel Hall (800 seats) is the primary facility on campus for large groups, concerts, distinguished guest lectures and films. Details concerning the use of these two halls is found in the **Policies Section.**

SECTION: IMS
SUBJECT: Audiovisual Services: General

35mm Photography and Slide Production:
The IMS photographs materials from books, still photographs and other sources to
make 35mm slides for classroom instruction. A turnaround time of two weeks is normal
for this service. Instant Polaroid slide service is available in an emergency situation or
if high contrast slides are desired to reproduce line drawings (1$ per slide). The IMS
is also able to duplicate 35mm slides and produce instant 3"x 5" Kodak color prints
from 35mm slides. A new service involves the creation of title and graphic slides on a
Macintosh computer by sending the slide information via modem to a slide service in
Texas. Slides can be produced overnight at a cost of $5 per slide with a six slide
minimum order. See the IMS Director for details. In addition, a 35mm SLR camera is
available for loan to faculty, students and administrators for academic pursuits.
Requests are handled by the Director on an individual basis, including instruction for
novices.

Audiovisual Equipment Delivery:
Given 24 hour prior notice (reservation either by telephone, memo or in person), IMS
student workers will loan, deliver, operate (if necessary) and pick up the following
types of AV equipment: 16mm film projectors, 35mm slide projectors, audiocassette
decks, phonographs, overhead projectors, opaque projectors, rolling carts,
videocassette recorders, video cameras, videodisc players, TV monitors, computer
and video projectors, open reel recorders, portable screens, high fidelity stereo
systems, and filmstrip projectors. Professors are welcome to pick up and return any of
the above mentioned equipment for classroom use whenever they are unable to
request an IMS delivery 24 hours in advance.

Audiovisual Production Service:
Instructional Media Services produces audio recordings of campus events. This
includes both monorecordings (of lectures, poetry readings and discussions) and
stereorecordings (of music concerts and recitals). Given sufficient notice the IMS will
arrange for the videotaping of a campus event (student presentation, guest lecture,
concert, etc.) by either using a camcorder or the sophisticated two camera production
cart, or training the client to use the camcorder his or herself to record the event.

The IMS also produces instructional videotapes for the campus on "how to",
simulation/role play, guided tours and "what-if" topics. Contact the Director of the IMS
if you have any questions or a project in mind. These programs may be a combination
of in-studio and on-location production. The College also has a recently formed
student cable television club (the IMS Director is the advisor) that produces
programing for the student body. (see **Video Services Section**)

Audiovisual Consultation Service:
The Director provides assistance as the resource person for copyright considerations
(infringement and/or legality) ; the location of non-print materials for rental or purchase
(the IMS stocks hundreds of film catalogs) ; planning video productions to illustrate
concepts and the integration of other non-print media into the curriculum, especially
the need for careful planning and an explanation of why non-print media is more

effective and how to best utilize it; and the purchase of A-V hardware in an effort to combine the resources of the college to ensure continued compatibility of equipment throughout the campus.

Audiovisual Equipment Repair and Maintainence Service:
The part-time IMS electronics technician is able to repair A-V equipment owned by the college at a cost well below that of outside service. Academic departments are urged to put all A-V equipment on a preventative maintenance schedule similar to the IMS program in order to avoid costly repair bills in the future. Consult the Director for details.

Source of Audiovisual Supplies:
The Media Center stocks the following items for the college, which departments are urged to utilize: transparency markers, audio and video recording tape, transparency film, slide trays, projector extension cords, and projection lamps. These items are purchased in sufficient quantity to allow for a substantial discount to the departments. Price information is available at IMS.

Related Audiovisual Services:
The IMS produces thermal transparencies for the professors, offers a dry mounting and laminating service, provides a 16 mm film splicing and repair service and acts as a clearinghouse for audiovisual catalogs and related materials.

SECTION: IMS
SUBJECT: IMS Policies

Planning Ahead:

In order to take best advantage of the variety of audiovisual services that **IMS** offers the campus, three things must be considered in order to avoid confusion when the time comes to utilize these services. PLAN AHEAD, PLAN AHEAD, and PLAN AHEAD. There are certain physical limitations to which types of equipment which can be used on certain parts of the campus and it is best to be aware of these limitations. The IMS Director can provide alternative solutions and/or suggest different media to accomplish the desired educational objective. Non-print utilization is encouraged and nurtured by the IMS, but of all of the factors to consider, pre-planning is the most critical (the most appropriate medium to accomplish the objective; is it available?, if not, where to find it; is the room suitable for the utilization of the desired media; etc)

Equipment Loan Policy:

Audiovisual equipment is purchased and maintained by Franklin and Marshall College in direct support of the Academic, Athletic and student affairs programs of the College. To this end, equipment may be used by faculty administrators and students for classroom presentations, individual scholarly endeavors, and recognized extracurricular activities. Equipment may not be borrowed for personal entertainment use nor removed from campus for use by community non-profit organizations or businesses. All loans to students must be supported by a request from a faculty member: in the case of student organizations, the advisor of that organization must assume responsibility for its prompt return; the correction of any damage in excess of normal wear is the responsibility of the borrower. Equipment loans and reservation are made on the basis of "equipment available"

Room Reservation Procedure:

If a member of the college community wishes to use a facility for audiovisual purposes at any time (or place) **other than their regularly scheduled class period (or room)**, they must do the following well in advance of the planned event:

1. contact the College Reservationist at 291-3858 to reserve the room
2. contact IMS and reserve the necessary audiovisual equipment

Two week's advance notice is the general rule to ensure that a facility will be available, but it would be wise to plan even further ahead for certain rooms such as Stahr, Hensel, or the College Center rooms. Absolutely no requests to reserve Hensel Hall or Stahr Auditorium will be accommodated with less than 48 hours notice ,and once again, two week's advance notice is the general rule   Specific guidelines for the reservation of other campus facilities may be found in the **facility reservation section** of this manual.

If a member of the faculty wishes to use audiovisual equipment in his or her regularly scheduled class and room, he or she needs to contact the IMS at their earliest convenience regarding if the IMS in fact has the necessary equipment and if it is available at the specified time. In general, one week's advance notice is greatly appreciated and will ensure the request is honored. No equipment will be delivered anywhere if less than 24 hours notice is given. Professors are more than welcome, in fact encouraged, to pick up and return equipment for classes themselves.

Copyright Policies:
The College maintains a library of videocassettes and video discs which are utilized in strict adherence to the Copyright Law Revision of 1976. Under section 110 of this law, the college is able to purchase and display video materials which bear the warning label " For Home Use Only" an utilize them for instructional purposes in support of the regular College curriculum.

Any questions regarding the Copyright Law or the Fair-Use Guidelines established by Congress in 1981 and Franklin and Marshall's adherence to the provisions concerning students viewing videocassettes should be directed to the Director of the Office of Instructional Media Services. In general, videocassettes may only be used for entertainment purposes if the copyright owner has granted expressed written permission for that purpose. The granting of such permission usually involves a fee.

A detailed explanation of the College Policy for the utilization of video materials and the College Policy for Duplication of Audiovisual Materials is found in the copyright section of this manual.

SECTION: IMS
SUBJECT: Audiovisual Services: Video

Before outlining the variety of video services the IMS offers the campus, some explanation about videocassette formats and equipment compatibility is needed. Videocassettes come in four basic varieties: 3/4" Umatic format;1/2" VHS format; 1/2" Beta format; and 8mm format. The 3/4", 1/2", and 8mm refer to the actual width of the recording tape. The UMATIC cassettes are much larger than either VHS, Beta or 8mm cassettes. 8mm cassettes, the smallest, are about the size of an audiocassette and fit in your shirt pocket. One obvious difference between Beta and VHS cassettes is that VHS cassettes have two windows you can see the tape through and Beta cassettes only have one window. Beta cassettes are also a bit smaller than VHS cassettes. F&M does not have any 8mm video equipment at the present time. 95% of the IMS video equipment is VHS format. VIDEOCASSETTE FORMATS ARE NOT INTERCHANGEABLE. Any questions about what type of videocassette you have of if the IMS has the equipment to play the cassette where you want it played should be directed to the IMS AS SOON AS POSSIBLE (ideally weeks in advance) so that other arrangements or alternative solutions may be suggested if we are unable to fulfill the request.

Source of Information on Films and Videos:
The Media Center has numerous catalogs of pre-recorded videotapes (usually cheaper than 16mm film) and, as a member of the Television Licensing Center, has information regarding PBS scheduling and which programs can legally be taped and kept for a cost far below the purchase price.

Satellite Television Earth Station:
The College recently installed a domestic satellite dish antenna capable of receiving a wide variety of television programs. F&M belongs to a consortium which makes otherwise unobtainable foreign language broadcasting available. Presently, we are receiving programming from Canada, Mexico, Germany, France, Italy, Austria, the Soviet Union, Poland, China, Japan, Spain, India, Israel, New Zealand, and Great Britain; as well as their U.S. based newscasters as they beam stories back to their home country in their native tongue. All requests for recording are handled by the IMS Director. There are also a vast array of science and educational programs now available. In addition, F&M could serve as a Host Site for a regional or national teleconference because the television signal can be directly broadcast into Stahr Auditorium and displayed on the seven foot video projection system. All copyright considerations and licensing questions are handled through the IMS Director. The IMS also stocks satellite programming guides so that professors can request specific programs.

Videocassette Duplication and Off-Air TV Recording for Professors:
According to the fair use doctrine (the latest copyright interpretation) a professor may use an off-air recording (videotape) in his classroom once for a period of up to ten consecutive school days after the program has been aired on network television, without copyright infringement. For the next thirty-five calendar days, (total time a tape may be kept is forty-five calendar days) said professor may keep the tape for private viewing in order to decide if it is worth keeping i.e., purchasing a license agreement to

keep it. After the forty-five day period is up, it is the professor's responsibility to either have the tape erased or contact the producer of the tape to obtain a license agreement. This process is done in cooperation with the director of the IMS. All off-air recording is done by the Director of the IMS and all off-air tapes are housed at the Media Center.

Video Production Service:
Given sufficient notice the IMS will arrange for the videotaping of a campus event (student presentation, guest lecture, concert, etc.) by either using a camcorder or the sophisticated two camera production cart, or training the client to use the camcorder his or herself to record the event.

The IMS also produces instructional videotapes for the campus on "how to", simulation/role play, guided tours and "what-if" topics. Contact the Director of the IMS if you have any questions or a project in mind. These programs may be a combination of in-studio and on-location production. The College also has a recently formed student cable television club (the IMS Director is the advisor) that produces programing for the student body.

FRANKLIN AND MARSHALL COLLEGE INSTRUCTIONAL MEDIA SERVICES

Media Services   **Fall 1987**

I. Video Services:

Presently the IMS offers the campus eight types of video services. Listed below is an outline of these services. Please stop by the Media Center, room 019 on the ground floor of Stahr Hall or call ext. 4019 (291-4019) if you have any questions as to how the IMS can best serve you. Our hours are Monday-Thursday 8AM-10PM; Friday 8AM-4:30PM and Sunday 1PM-10PM.

A. **Videocassette playback:** (an individual or group can watch a pre-recorded videocassette)

1. 1/2" VHS format
2. 1/2" BETA format
3. 3/4" UMATIC format

A rolling AV cart with a videocassette recorder (VCR) and a TV monitor can be set up in most classroom buildings. This is ideal for groups of less than a dozen. A portable projection television system which produces a six-foot wide image is available for larger groups. Professors may also schedule S-102, the 170-seat auditorium in Stahr Hall which has a rear screen projection system for video, computer data, 16mm film and 35mm slides; as well as an electronic overhead projector for transparencies or any opaque material needed to illustrate a point. Students and professors can also take advantage of the four carrels equipped with televisions and VHS format VCR's housed in the listening facility (Media Center) to view videocassettes at their leisure. This provides an excellent way to preview materials, complete remedial work, or catch up on missed assignments. Professors may also assign students to watch videocassettes in the Media Center on their own time (as is now the practice for audiocassettes).

1

B. Videodisc playback: (an individual or group can watch a pre-recorded laser videodisc)

The IMS can only play laser optical videodiscs. (CED discs, made by the RCA Corporation, will not work in our units) See the IMS Director for any further explanation. All videocassette viewing options apply for videodiscs, including watching discs in the Media Center.

C. Satellite Television Downlink Earth Station:

The College recently installed a domestic satellite dish antenna capable of receiving a wide variety of television programs. F&M belongs to a consortium which makes otherwise unobtainable foreign language broadcasting available. Presently, we are receiving programming from Canada, Mexico, Germany, France, Italy, Austria, the Soviet Union, Poland, China, Japan, Spain, Israel, New Zealand, and Great Britain; as well as their U.S. based newscasters as they beam stories back to their home country in their native tongue. All requests for recording are handled by the IMS Director. There are also a vast array of science and educational programs now available. In addition, F&M could serve as a Host Site for a regional or national teleconference because the television signal can be directly broadcast into Stahr Auditorium and displayed on the seven foot video projection system. All copyright considerations and licensing questions are handled through the IMS Director.

D. Videocassette duplication and off-air (TV) recording
for F&M professors (copyright permitting):

According to the fair use doctrine (the latest copyright interpretation) a professor may use an off-air recording (videotape) in his classroom once for a period of up to ten consecutive school days after the program has been aired on network television, without copyright infringement. For the next thirty-five calendar days, (total time a tape may be kept is forty-five calendar days) said professor may keep the tape for private viewing in order to decide if it is worth keeping i.e., purchasing a license agreement to keep it. After the forty-five day period is up, it is the professor's responsibility to either have the tape erased or contact the producer of the tape to obtain a license agreement. This process is done in cooperation with the director of the IMS. All off-air recording is done by the director of the IMS and all off-air tapes are housed at the Media Center.

2

E. **Record a live campus event on videotape:** (student presentation, guest lecture, critique of teaching style, etc.)

F. **Large screen personal computer display for classroom presentations:** (using the very portable and easy to use Limelight Projector, the IMS can link a Macintosh or IBM-PC with a computer projection system to create a six-foot wide representation of what is on your IBM or Macintosh monitor. Departments which heavily utilize the Macintosh in their classes may have a computer projector in their department on a long term basis....call the IMS Director for details.)

G. **Videotape search (purchase or rental):**
The Media Center has numerous catalogs of pre-recorded tapes (usually cheaper than 16mm film) and, as a member of the Television Licensing Center, has information regarding PBS scheduling and which programs can legally be taped and kept for a cost far below the purchase price.

H. **Videotape Production:**
The IMS produces instructional videotapes for the campus on "how to", simulation/role play, guided tours and "what-if" topics. Contact the Director of the IMS if you have any questions or a project in mind.

A WORD ABOUT FORMATS

Videocassettes come in four basic varieties: 3/4" Umatic format; 1/2" VHS format; 1/2" Beta format; and 8mm format. The 3/4", 1/2", and 8mm refer to the actual width of the recording tape. The UMATIC cassettes are much larger than either VHS, Beta or 8mm cassettes. 8mm cassettes, the smallest, are about the size of an audiocassette and fit in your shirt pocket. One obvious difference between Beta and VHS cassettes is that VHS cassettes have two windows you can see the tape through and Beta cassettes only have one window. Beta cassettes are also a bit smaller than VHS cassettes. F&M does not have any 8mm video equipment at the present time. 95% of the IMS video equipment is VHS format. VIDEOCASSETTE FORMATS ARE NOT INTERCHANGEABLE.

3

II.   35mm SLIDE PRODUCTION SERVICE :

The IMS photographs materials from books, still photographs
and other sources to make 35mm slides for classroom
instruction. A turnaround time of two weeks is normal for this
service. Instant Polaroid slide service is available in an
emergency situation or if high contrast slides are desired to
reproduce line drawings (1$ per slide). The IMS is also able to
duplicate 35mm slides and produce instant 3"x 5" Kodak color
prints from 35mm slides.

III.   35mm PHOTOGRAPHY:

A 35mm SLR camera is available for loan to faculty, students
and administrators for academic pursuits. Requests are
handled by the Director on an individual basis, including
instruction for novices.

IV.   AUDIO VISUAL EQUIPMENT LOAN, DELIVERY AND
PICK UP SERVICE:
Student workers will loan, deliver, operate (if necessary) and
pick up the following types of AV equipment: 16mm film
projectors, 35mm slide projectors, audiocassette decks,
phonographs, overhead projectors, opaque projectors, rolling
carts, videocassette recorders, video cameras, videodisc
players, TV monitors, computer and video projectors, open
reel recorders, portable screens, high fidelity stereo systems,
and filmstrip projectors.

V.   AUDIO TAPE PRODUCTION SERVICE AND AUDIO LISTENING
FACILITY:

The IMS service includes high speed cassette duplication of
foreign language tapes, transfer of materials from records and
open reel tapes onto cassettes, maintaining the audio cassette
inventory and the operation of the twenty carrel audio cassette
listening facility. The following departments have
audiocassettes filed in the Media Center library: American
Studies, Biology, Drama, English, French, German, Italian,
Music, Portuguese, Religious Studies, Russian, Sociology., and
Spanish. The Media Center now houses fifteen stereo
audiocassette listening carrels, two mono audiocassette carrels,
five stereo high fidelity (phonograph) stations, and three
compact disc players for the students' listening. Modern
language professors may also assign dictation exercises for
students to complete at the Media Center.

4

VI.   AUDIO VISUAL CONSULTATION SERVICE:

The Director provides assistance as the resource person for copyright considerations (infringement and/or legality) ; the location of non-print materials for rental or purchase (the IMS stocks hundreds of film catalogs) ; planning video productions to illustrate concepts and the integration of other non-print media into the curriculum, especially the need for careful planning and an explanation of why non-print media is more effective and how to best utilize it; and the purchase of A-V hardware in an effort to combine the resources of the college to ensure continued compatibility of equipment throughout the campus.

VII.   FRANKLIN AND MARSHALL PHONOGRAPH RECORD AND COMPACTDISC COLLECTION:

The F&M record collection is housed in Stahr Hall. High fidelity stereo turntables and compactdisc players are located there for listening purposes. **Records are no longer circulated.** Exception: professors may sign out records for a class or campus production. They should be returned immediately afterward.

VIII.   EQUIPMENT REPAIR AND MAINTENANCE SERVICE:

The IMS technician is able to repair A-V equipment owned by the college at a cost well below that of outside service. Academic departments are urged to put all A-V equipment on a preventative maintenance schedule similar to the IMS program in order to avoid costly repair bills in the future. Consult the Director for details.

IX.   SOURCE OF AUDIO VISUAL SUPPLIES:

The Media Center stocks the following items for the college, which departments are urged to utilize: transparency markers, audio and video recording tape, transparency film, slide trays, projector extension cords, and projection lamps. These items are purchased in sufficient quantity to allow for a substantial discount to the departments.

5

X.   RELATED AUDIO VISUAL SERVICES:

The IMS produces thermal transparencies for the professors, offers a dry mounting and laminating service, provides a film splicing and repair service and acts as a clearinghouse for audio visual catalogs and related materials. The Media Center houses various F&M 35mm slide collections and has a carrel- mounted 35mm slide Caramate projector to view slides. The Media Center also has a carrel-mounted 16mm film projectors professor and students can use for previewing films in the Media Center.

FRANKLIN AND MARSHALL COLLEGE
INSTRUCTIONAL MEDIA SERVICES

EQUIPMENT LOAN POLICY

Audio visual equipment is purchased and maintained by Franklin and Marshall College in direct support of the Academic, Athletic and student affairs programs of the College. To this end, equipment may be used by faculty administrators and students for classroom presentations, individual scholarly endeavors, and recognized extracurricular activities. Equipment may not be borrowed for personal entertainment use nor removed from campus for use by community non-profit organizations or businesses. All loans to students must be supported by a request from a faculty member: in the case of student organizations, the advisor of that organization must assume responsibility for its prompt return; the correction of any damage in excess of normal wear is the responsibility of the borrower. Equipment loans and reservation are made on the basis of "equipment available"

6

[This document has been retyped to improve legibility.]

FRANKLIN AND MARSHALL COLLEGE
Interoffice Memorandum   August 13, 1986

TO: The Faculty and Administration

FROM: Dean Dewey

RE: College Policy for Using Videocassettes and Video Discs

Jon Enos, Director of Instructional Media Services, continues to keep us alert to the legal ramifications of using the new technology in his field.

Attached is Jon's summary of proper legal use of videocassettes and video discs. This summary is College policy on these matters. If you have questions of interpretation, please contact Jon.

TO: The Faculty and Administration   August 13, 1986

FROM: Jonathan Enos, Director, Instructional Media Services [JE]

RE: College Policy for Using Videocassettes and Video Discs

The College maintains a library of videocassettes and video discs which are utilized in adherence to the Copyright Law Revision of 1976. Under section 110 of this law, the College is able to purchse and display video materials which bear the warning label "For Home Use Only". However, there are significant limitatins to how the College may utilize such video materials. The College strictly abides by the limitations listed below. The word "display" means to show individual images nonsequentially from a videocassette and the word "performance" means to show the images of a videocassete in any sequence or to make the sounds accompanying it audible.1

Section 110 of the 1976 Copyright Law "Limitations on Exclusive Rights: Exemption of Certain Performances and Displays" authorizes a wide variety of performances and displays in face-to-face teaching, but it imposes some significant limitations. All of the six conditions listed below must be met in order for it to be a legal use of a videocassette.

1. Performances and displays of audiovisual works (films, videocassettes, etc.) must be made from legitimate copies;

2. performances and displays must take place in a classroom or similar place devoted to instruction and not transmitted by broadcast or cable television;

3. performances and displays must be part of a systematic course of instruction and not for entertainment, recreation or cultural value;

4. performances and displays must be given by the instructors or pupils;

5. performances and displays must be part of the teaching activities of a nonprofit educational institution; and

6. attendance at performances and displays is limited to the instructor, pupils and guest lecturers.2

While all are important and must be satisfied, the key conditions are one and three. Condition number one states the videocassette must be legally obtained in order to be used in the classroom; therefore, while a professor (as well as any individual) may tape a television program off-air and use it in the privacy of the home, he or she is forbidden by law to use that videocassette in the classroom (unless it is within ten days of the broadcast date as per the fair-use exemption). Condition number three states the video must be part of systematic instrucitonal activities (i.e. incorporated into the curriculum of a regularly scheduled course) and not be used for entertainment or cultural purposes, no matter how valid the cultural aspects of the program may be.

Any questions regarding the Copyright Law or the Fair-Use Guidelines established by Congress in 1981 and Franklin and Marshall's adherence to the provisions concerning students viewing videocassettes should be directed tothe Director of the Office of Instrucitonal Media Services. It should be noted that videocassettes may be used for entertainment purposes if the copyright owner has granted permission for the person or group on campus requesting to use said videocassette. These licenses must be applied for in writing and usually require a fee.

1. United States Code, Title 17, "Copyrights," Section 101.

2. Miller, Jerome K., Using Copyrighted Videocassettes in Classrooms and Libraries," 1984, page 24.

74

[This document has been retyped to improve legibility.]

FRANKLIN AND MARSHALL COLLEGE
Interoffice Memorandum   August 15, 1984

TO: The Faculty and Administration

FROM: Dean Dewey [BAD]

RE: Summary of College Policy for Duplication of Audio
           Visual Materials

The College has adopted the attached "Summary of College
Policy for Duplication of Audio Visual Materials." Much has
changed with respect to video copyright guidelines since the
College's most recent 1980 Policy Statement. Once again the
College solicitor was consulted. He interpreted the legal
doctrine of the "Guidelines for Off-Air Recording of Broadcast
Programming for Educational Purposes" which was adopted by
Congress in 1981 and he made recommendations accordingly. These
guidelines, commonly known as the fair-use guidelines, form the
basis for the College's revised videotaping policy. The
guidelines also carry the force of law and the law provides for
substantial penalties for noncompliance, as evidenced by the
recent (1983) decision in the Encyclopedia Britannica versus the
Board of Cooperative Services (BOCES) of Buffalo, NY. The judge
found the defendant BOCES guilty of copyright infringement as a
result of the illegal off-air videotaping fothe works of
plaintiffs whose copyrights were owned by them. The fuling will
cost the BOCES upwards of $400,000. It is the aim of the College
to comply with Copyright Law and the fair-use guidelines while
continuing to make use of the vast resources of audio visual
materials available.

Any questions arising from the guidelines may be handled in
the following ways: individuals may consult the complete
guidelines (on file in the Library, the AVLC and the Office of
the Dean of the College) to clarify areas of particular interest;
specific questions of policy or procedure should be addressed to
Jon Enos, Director of Audio Visual Learning Center; interest in
general faculty discussion of the guidelines may be addressed to
the Faculty Meeting Agenda Committee.

jg

Guidelines for the Duplication of
Records, Tapes and Sound Tracks
of Audiovisual Works

1. A record or tape (hereafter referred to as sound recordings) which does not bear a Notice of Copyright is not subject to copyright protection and may be duplicated in whole or in part for instructional or research purposes.

2. A sound recording which is subject to copyright protection will bear on its label or container a Notice of Copyright which employs the symbol Ⓟ . For example:

   Ⓟ   1974 Ace Music Co.

3. A sound recording which is subject to copyright protection may be duplicated for instructional or research purposes in accordance with the rules set forth in paragraphs 4 through 6 below.

4. A foreign language sound recording which is not produced or marketed for purposes of teaching a foreign language may be duplicated in whole or in part and the resulting copies may be retained and used for purposes of foreign language instruction.

5. A foreign language sound recording produced or marketed for purposes of foreign language instruction, an English language sound recording of a dramatic or literary work, or a sound recording of a musical work may be duplicated only as follows:

   A. A sound recording which is not commercially available may be duplicated in whole or in part. For example, a sound recording of a performance by Karajan of Beethoven's Symphony No. 5 may be duplicated if it cannot be obtained from commercial sources, even though a sound recording of that work by another artist may be commercially available.

   B. In the case of a sound recording which is owned by the College and which is presently available from commercial sources, one complete copy may be produced for each original owned by the College for purposes of changing the recording into a more desirable format. (For example, a record may be duplicated by recording a copy on reel-to-reel tape.) Small portions of such a recording may also be duplicated.

   C. In the case of a sound recording which has been rented by the College, one complete copy may be produced for purposes of changing the recording into a more desirable format, provided that the copy is erased at the end of the rental period. A small portion of a rented sound recording may be duplicated and the resulting copies may be retained for future use.

OVER

D. A sound recording which has been loaned to the College may be duplicated in its entirety only if an original cannot be commercially obtained. A small portion of a borrowed sound recording may be duplicated and the resulting copies may be retained for future use.

E. A "small portion" is, as a general rule, 10% or less of a sound recording.

6. The following sound recordings, if subject to copyright protection, may not be duplicated:

A. A sound recording which has been obtained on a "for approval" basis.

B. A sound recording which is commercially available and which is intended for sale principally to students for individual use.

7. A sound track of an audiovisual work (a motion picture, vidoetape or narrated filmstrip, for example) may be duplicated for instructional or research purposes as follows:

A. A foreign language sound track of an audiovisual work which is not produced or marketed for purposes of teaching a foreign language may be duplicated in whole or in part and the resulting copies may be retained and used for purposes of foreign language instruction.

B. A sound track of an audiovisual work produced or marketed for purposes of foreign language instruction or a sound track of a musical or English language audiovisual work may be duplicated in accordance with the rules applicable to sound recordings as set forth in paragraphs 4 through 6 above.

8. In any case where duplication of a sound recording or sound track is permitted, the number of copies produced may not exceed the minimum number required to satisfy the particular need.

Guidelines for the
Production of Transperencies

1. Subject to the caveat of paragraph 2, a single transparency may be made of any work appearing in a book, pamphlet or similar publication which is owned by the College. For example, in the case of an art book which contains 50 prints, one transparency of each print may be produced.

2. Works appearing in books, pamphlets and similar publications intended for sale principally to students for individual use may not be reproduced unless the publication involved is not commercially available for sale.

3. Works appearing in books, pamphlets and similar publications which have been loaned to the College by another institution may not be reproduced unless the publication involved is not commercially available for sale. In the case of a publication which is not commercially available for sale, the College may make a single transparency of any work appearing in that publication.

4. In the case of a periodical, a single transparency may be made of any work appearing in a particular issue of a periodical if the College owns the issue, if the issue is not commercially available for sale, or if the College subscribes to the periodical involved.

5. Transparencies produced in accordance with these guidelines may be catalogued and retained indefinitely, provided that they are used exclusively for purposes of research and classroom instruction. Transparencies which have been lost, damaged, or destroyed may be replaced by making a new transparency.

OVER

Guidelines for Off-Air Recording of Broadcast Programming for Educational Purposes

The following guidelines, which form the basis for the Franklin and Marshall College Videotaping Guidelines, are taken directly from "The Congressional Record - extensions of remarks," October 14, 1981 page E4750. Drafted by a subcommittee negotiating team which was chaired by Congressman Robert Kastenmeier and included representatives from all sides of the issue, the guidelines were subsequently adopted by the United States Congress.

1. The guidelines were developed to apply only to off-air recording by non-profit educational institutions.

2. A broadcast program may be recorded off-air simultaneously with broadcast transmission, including simultaneous cable retransmission, and retained by a non-profit educational institution for a period not to exceed the first forty-five consecutive calendar days after the date of recording. Upon conclusion of such retention period, all off-air recordings must be erased or destroyed immediately. (The only exception being if the producer of the program has been contacted in writing within the 45-day period by the institution requesting a license to legally retain the tape for future instructional use and said producer has consented to such a license agreement.) "Broadcast programs" are television programs transmitted by television stations for reception by the general public without charge.

3. Off-air recordings may be used once by individual teachers in the course of relevant teaching activities, and repeated only once when instructional reinforcement is necessary, in classrooms and similar places devoted to instruction within a single building, cluster or campus, as well as in the homes of students receiving formalized home instruction, during the first ten consecutive school days in the forty-five calendar day retention period. "School days" are school session days—not counting weekends, holidays, vacations, examination periods, or other scheduled interruptions—within the forty-five day retention period.

4. Off-air recordings may be made only at the request of and used by individual teachers, and may not be regularly recorded (by the audio visual department) in anticipation of requests. No broadcast program may be recorded off-air more than once at the request of the same teacher, regardless of the number of times the program may be broadcast.

5. A limited number of copies may be reproduced from each off-air recording to meet the legitimate needs of teachers under these guidelines. Each additional copy shall be subject to all provisions governing the original recording.

6. After the first ten consecutive school days, off-air recordings may be used up to the end of the forty-five calendar retention period only for teacher evaluation broadcast program in the teaching curriculum (or to obtain an off-air license agreement from the producer if one is available), and may not be used in the recording institution or any other non-evaluation purpose without authorization.

7. Off-air recordings need not be used in their entirety, but the recorded programs may not be altered from their original content. Off-air recordings may not be physically or electronically combined or merged to constitute teaching anthologies or compilations.

8. All copies of off-air recordings must include the copyright notice on the broadcast program as recorded.

9. Educational institutions are expected to establish appropriate control procedures to maintain the integrity of these guidelines.

FRANKLIN AND MARSHALL COLLEGE VIDEOTAPING GUIDELINES

In addition to the above mentioned guidelines, Franklin and Marshall College's videotaping policy includes the following:

1. All requests for videotaping television programs should be sent to the Director of the AVLC who shall review each request in order to determine whether the program involved may be recorded consistently with the terms of this Statement of Policy.

2. The only television programs F & M may record are those which are broadcast by television stations to the viewer free of charge. F & M may not record programs which can only be received by the viewer upon payment of a fee (i.e., HBO or PRISM programs).

3. All off-air recording is to be done by the Director of the AVLC in strict accordance with the terms of this Statement of Policy. The use of such recordings is limited to purposes of preview, class use and evaluation. Furthermore, videotape recordings of television broadcasts prepared by the Audio Visual Learning Center may be used only by members of the College community for purposes of research or for purposes of classroom instruction in connection with an accredited academic course, and may not under any circumstances be loaned to other institutions or to persons not affiliated with the College.

4. The use of off-air recordings is additionally restricted to educational—not entertainment—purposes; all to be utilized on campus.

OVER

5. Videotape playback equipment owned by the College may be used for purposes of replaying a videotape of a television broadcast only if that videotape recording was prepared by the Audio Visual Learning Center or produced by and obtained from a legitimate commercial enterprise.

6. A log of all off-air recordings will be kept by the Director of the AVLC. This log will include the following: title and source of the program; date and time recorded; who requested the recording; who recorded it; where and when it was shown on campus; the erasure date (end of the 45-day retention period); whether the program was erased or a license agreement was obtained.

7. All off-air recordings will be kept by the Director of the AVLC until they are either erased or a license agreement is obtained by the professor who requested the program be taped. The professor is responsible for obtaining the license agreement from the producer of the program.

8. The Director of the AVLC will provide licensing information to all requesting professors. The license application must be made (and subsequent approval obtained) by the professors (the AVLC Director will assist). THE DIRECTOR OF THE AVLC MUST BE SENT THE COMPLETED LICENSE AGREEMENT (accepted by the producer and paid for by the College) WITHIN THE 45-DAY RETENTION PERIOD OR HE WILL BE FORCED TO ERASE THE TAPE.

9. All arrangements for showing off-air recordings will be made through the AVLC.

10. These guidelines are designed to ensure F & M's strict adherence to the fair-use guidelines of the copyright law.

jg

HOLLINS COLLEGE

Hollins College
Fishburn Library
Audio Visual Department

AV ACQUISITIONS POLICY

1. Audiovisual services are an adjunct to the general services of the Fishburn Library. Its goals and purposes are those of the Library: to support and enhance the educational mission of the College by acquiring, storing and making available for use those non-book materials necessary to the curriculum and the undergraduate cultural experience. Making available for use implies supplying the mechanical equipment needed to display and transmit images and data stored in non-book form to classrooms and other campus environments.

2. In terms of recorded sound, it will not be the purpose of the Library to replicate or rival the comprehensive, non-circulating collections maintained by the Music Department. The Library's priorities will be:

   a. locally generated recordings of lectures, readings, and concerts, including student productions and campus activities;

   b. the spoken word, including drama, poetry in all languages, and language teaching and other instructional materials;

   c. representative folk music from various times and cultures, particularly that related to bardic and balladic traditions;

   d. music in a theatrical setting; that is, opera, ballet, and musical comedy;

   e. a basic circulating collection of classical standards;

   f. music illustrative of the evolution of popular taste and recording technology.

3. Priorities for the acquisition of films, videotapes, and videodiscs will be:

   a. locally generated films and tapes as in 2a;

   b. feature films, documentaries, and educational films requested by members of the teaching faculty for curriculum-related purposes;

85

c.   a basic library of feature films beyond immediate curriculum needs, illustrative of the evolution of popular taste and cinema art, using as guides standard film histories, critical reviews, consensus critical judgement, and suggestions from members of the College community;

d.   in keeping with the Library's policies for printed materials, a margin of materials for recreational use.

4.   Nothing in the foregoing should be interpreted to restrict the Library from soliciting or accepting gifts or bequests which, although not included in the stated priorities, might contribute significantly to the College's educational mission.

5.   In the acquisition and use of the audiovisual materials, and with particular reference to video formats, it is not the intent of the Library in any way to compete with movie theatres or local retail outlets. Except as dictated by the stated priorities, therefore, current popularity will be a negative consideration.

6.   In the acquisition and use of audiovisual materials, the Library will strictly observe all applicable copyright restrictions.

Draft
Richard Kirkwood 7/90

JOHN CARROLL UNIVERSITY

JOHN CARROLL UNIVERSITY
AUDIO VISUAL DEPARTMENT

POLICIES AND PROCEDURES

FOR

OFF—AIR VIDEO RECORDING

GENERAL

The Audio Visual Department will support the instructional use of video programs recorded off—air within limits permitted by interpretations of the copyright law. These policies are intended to provide needed instructional materials which fall within the "fair use" guidelines of the copyright law without infringing upon the reasonable rights of the copyright holder. These guidelines apply only to off—air recording by non-profit, educational institutions and are as follows:

POLICIES

1. Programs will be recorded off—air only upon request of individual faculty. Programs will not be recorded for speculative use.

2. If a program is to be used within ten school days of its recording, it will be used without seeking copyright permission.

3. After the first 10 school days, off—air recordings may be used up to the 45 day limit only for teacher evaluation purposes and may not be used for student exhibition or any other non-evaluation purpose without permission.

4. A program may be recorded off—air simultaneously with broadcast transmission (including simultaneous cable re-transmission) and retained for a period not to exceed 45 calendar days after date of recording. Upon conclusion of such retention period, all off—air recordings will be erased unless permission to retain has been granted.

5. All copies of off—air recordings will include the copyright notice on the broadcast program as recorded.

6. If the educational use of a program is projected to take place more than ten days following the broadcast, copyright permission will be sought. The program will be recorded and the tape will be held pending approval for use.

7. If no response is received from the copyright holder within two weeks a second request for permission will be sent. If no response is received within two weeks of the second request it will be assumed that the program can be

used for instructional purposes.

8. If permission for use is denied by the copyright holder
the tape will be erased.

9. If the copyright holder seeks a licensing fee the fee
will be paid by the Audio Visual Dept. if it can be
accommodated by the current operating budget.

10. All off-air copying is subject to limitations of
existing Audio Visual Dept. equipment.

PROCEDURES

1. All requests by faculty and staff will be made 5 days
prior to the scheduled broadcast. Requests shall be directed
to the Audio Visual Dept.

2. Audio Visual Dept. personnel will determine any recording
restrictions which may be in effect at the time of the
request which may restrict or prohibit off-air recording or
subsequent use of programs.

3. If a program is to be used within 10 school days from the
broadcast date and off-air recording is not known to be
restricted, arrangements will be made at the time of request
for recording, playback and erasure.

4. If the program is to be used more than 10 school days
following broadcast, arrangements will be made for recording
and the Audio Visual Department will initiate a request for
use to the copyright holder.

5. The Audio Visual Dept. will maintain a file of permission
requests. If no response is received within 2 weeks a
second request will be sent to the copyright holder. If no
response is received within 2 weeks of the second request the
tape will be available for use.

6. If a licensing fee is required the agreement must be
reviewed by the Library Director. If the fee can be
accommodated by the current operating budget a requisition
for payment will be issued. If the fee requested exceeds
budget limitations, the using department will be contacted
regarding the feasibility of cost sharing. If it is decided
not to pay the licensing fee the copyright holder will be
notified and the tape in question will be erased.

7. Tapes recorded off-air will be housed and/or circulated
via the Library for educational use.

8. A file of all off-air recording transactions will be maintained by the Audio-Visual Dept. to include record of requests, recordings, playbacks and copyright permissions.

AUDIO VISUAL DEPARTMENT

VIDEO TAPING REQUEST

TITLE   SOURCE   LENGTH   DATE   TIME AIRED

I have requested the Audio Visual Department to video tape or duplicate, in it's entirety or in part, the above program(s), or tape(s).

I am seeking the duplication rights for the work listed above. It is further understood that any liability for copyright violation rests solely with myself and not with the Audio Visual Dept. or any of it's agents.

All recordings are subject to the availability of personnel.

Duplication charges and supplies are the responsibility of the department making the request.

Signature:_____

Department:_____

Date:_____
Budget No:_____
Fee:_____

92

M E M O R A N D U M

November 2, 1989

MEMO TO: JCU FACULTY

FROM: John Piety, Director, Grasselli Library

SUBJECT: **WHAT CAN AUDIO VISUAL SERVICES DO FOR ME?**

1.- EQUIPMENT AND OPERATOR SCHEDULING:
2.- FILM AND VIDEO SCHEDULING:
3.- OVERHEAD PROJECTOR SLIDE SUPPLIES:
4.- OFF-AIR RECORDING OF TV PROGRAMS:
5.- SPECIAL EQUIPMENT AVAILABLE:
   A. COMPUTER PROJECTION UNITS
   B. PAL/SECAM VCR FOR CONVERSION OR USE:
   C. SLIDE PROJECTORS
   D. SOUND EQUIPPED LECTERNS
   E. MINICAM VIDEO CAMERA/RECORDER
   F. AUDIOCASSETTE RECORDERS
   G. VARIABLE SPEED PHONOGRAPH/AMPLIFIER
   H. PORTABLE VIDEO PROJECTION UNIT
6.- AV SUPPLIES (BULBS, ETC.) AND REPAIR:
7.- STUDENT USE OF EQUIPMENT AND SERVICES:
8.- OFF CAMPUS USE OF EQUIPMENT:

Four years ago, the Audio-Visual Services department was turned over to the library to administer. Since that time, use of A-V resources has mushroomed, doubling each year. This memo will give you some idea of the equipment and services available through the A-V Services department. Please retain this for future reference. From time to time updates will detail new equipment and services or unique uses of the service. The charge to the library was to optimize use of expensive equipment and expensive materials so that each department would not be forced to purchase items which would be used only occasionally, and to make these high cost items available to all on a scheduled basis. Many departments have A-V equipment, few have enough to serve all their needs. Sometimes department equipment needs service or repair, and the A-V Services department can often fix broken equipment right here; if it needs to be sent out, a loaner can be given usually.

EQUIPMENT AND OPERATOR SCHEDULING:
Call ext. 4710 to schedule equipment or materials. We need five working days lead time to guarantee delivery of equipment or services. If you call on short notice, we will try to help, but cannot guarantee availability. Equipment is kept in the Recplex, Bohannon Science Building, Grasselli Library, and the Administration Building for rapid deployment. Be sure to specify the exact equipment, i.e. 16mm projector, not just projector. We have 35mm slide projectors, overhead projectors, etc. and don't want to deliver the wrong equipment. If you need a vcr, specify Beta, VHS, or 3/4 inch U-Matic. The best way to ensure accuracy is to fill out one of our forms for each use.

Page 1

FILM AND VIDEO SCHEDULING:
    To keep costs low, we always try our free sources first. Through
a contract with the Kent State University Audio Visual Department, you
can use any of their materials without charge. This is the largest
collection of academic videocassettes and films in the state. See your
department secretary to consult the new catalog and to find out the
specific delivery requirements. Other free sources are the Cleveland
Public Library and Cuyahoga County Public Library. Catalogs for these
sources are held at the circulation desk in the library. NOTE: These
public libraries are strict on borrowing the day before and returning
the day after use - a five dollar per day fine will be charged. If
none of the three mentioned have the title needed, the next source to
check is the FILM LOCATOR, a two volume listing kept at the circulation
desk. It lists AV materials available from fifty academic collections
nationwide. Usually a rental fee is charged by the lender. If you
know of a source, please list it on the form for ordering materials. A
special caveat: it is seldom legal to rent from a video store for
classroom showing. For clarification, contact Mr. Piety.

OVERHEAD PROJECTOR TRANSPARENCY SUPPLIES:
    The AV department on the third floor of the Administration
Building has supplies for making your own overhead transparencies.
They are sold at cost, and can be charged to your department. For
instruction on making the transparencies, call Dr. Dague of the
Education Department.

OFF-AIR RECORDING OF TELEVISION PROGRAMS:
    The department can make recordings of current programs for you.
Within the copyright guidelines, a copy can be made of any program
available on the VIACOM cable network. The AV department can also
duplicate videocassettes and audiocassettes, within the copyright
guidelines. A copy of our Policies and Procedures guide is attached.
If you are unsure of copyright provisions, contact Mr. Piety.

SPECIAL EQUIPMENT AVAILABLE:
    A. COMPUTER PROJECTION UNITS. We have two portable projection
units, (SHARP QA-50) which fit on an overhead projector and handle an
image up to 10 feet on a side for classroom viewing. They work best in
rooms that can be darkened. They are most effective with our new
overhead projectors which are brighter than some of the older units.
For black and white images in the classroom they work very well. If
color is required, the Mackin Lecture Room has a projection unit that
handles color, but it cannot be moved to classrooms.

    B. PAL/SECAM VCR FOR CONVERSION OR USE. More videotapes in foreign
formats are becoming available. We have a unit to show or copy from
the European and Japanese formats to standard VHS cassettes or to
display the materials on screen.

    C. SLIDE PROJECTORS. We have a number of carousel projectors for
classroom use, and a dissolve unit, fader, etc. for use as needed in
multi-projector presentations. There are some special purpose
projectors we can call on as needed for unique jobs.

    D. SOUND EQUIPPED LECTERNS. We have three sound equipped lecterns
useful when amplification is needed in the classroom or out of doors.

Page 2

94

Each is equipped with a power cord, but they can run on batteries for a time if the nearest plug is too far away. Specify if you need the battery power so we can put in the batteries.

E. MINICAM VIDEO CAMERA/RECORDER. One unit is on order and should arrive this semester. It will be available as soon as we can get it.

F. AUDIOCASSETTE RECORDERS. We have several hand held audiocassette recorders that can be checked out for special uses. In addition, the former phonograph listening room in Grasselli Library now has cassette players replacing three of the old phonograph listening stations.

G. VARIABLE SPEED PHONOGRAPH/AMPLIFIER. In Grasselli Library there is a variable speed phonograph setup that is often useful in special cases. It is most often used within the library, so if you need to take it outside the library, contact the director.

H. PORTABLE VIDEO PROJECTION UNIT. We have a portable video projector on order, due to arrive this semester. It is one of the new generation machines and offers great advantages over the old BARCO units. You will be notified when it is available.

AV SUPPLIES (BULBS ETC.) AND REPAIR:
    We keep on hand the bulbs and other small parts needed for AV equipment. In some cases we can help a department with a quick onsite replacement bulb, belt, etc. Jim Molnar can make minor repairs on most equipment on campus. Major repairs are sent out to service agencies. In some cases, if a department machine must be sent out, we can provide a "loaner" for a short time. This depends on availability of equipment and.scheduling of use.

STUDENT USE OF EQUIPMENT AND SERVICES:
    Students who need equipment or films, videocassettes, etc. for classroom presentations can request items in the same fashion as our faculty and staff. We encourage student use of the materials and equipment for presentations. This does not mean checking out gear for private use in dorms or at home.

OFF CAMPUS USE OF EQUIPMENT:
    Generally speaking, any of the equipment can be used off campus for university needs. For example, a vcr could be checked out to use at Carrollodge or Thornacres; or for a university function in a local church or other meeting place. As always, scheduling of equipment for on campus use comes first. I the equipment won't come back in time for a scheduled use it cannot be taken off campus.

    None of the above is set in stone. If you need services or equipment that is not available, contact the library director and we'll see what can be done.

1 attch: Off-Air video recording policies and procedures.

Page 3

KALAMAZOO COLLEGE

Audio Services

Audiotapes of campus events and performances can be recorded and audio recordings duplicated for archival, instructional, and individual use in compliance with copyright regulations.

Language Lab

The center staff administers the language lab in Dewing Hall in cooperation with the foreign language faculty.

Video Services

The Fetzer Media Center provides limited off-the-air taping, tape duplication, and editing services in compliance with copyright guidelines. Briefly stated, they are:

> A program may be videotaped at the time of broadcast if specifically requested; programs may not be taped routinely in anticipation of requests.
>
> A taped program may be shown *once* for classroom use and may be retained for evaluation purposes for 45 calendar days.

The center staff will videotape presentations by students and faculty for instructional purposes. Arrangements must be made in advance.

Video playback equipment (¾" and ½" VHS) can be scheduled for classroom use in Dewing Hall, Upjohn Library, Light Fine Arts Building, Anderson Athletic Center, and the Stryker Center.

Fees and Fines

Fees for instructional users cover the cost of supplies. The fee schedule for non-instructional units of the college and for community groups is available at the media center office.

To encourage prompt return, fines are charged for all overdue equipment and materials. Fines accumulate until the item is returned, renewed, declared lost, or until the fine reaches $10.

Materials. . . . . $.05 per day
Audiovisual equipment. . . . . $1.00 first hour
$.25 per hour thereafter

Fetzer
Communications
Media Center

Kalamazoo College
Library & Media
Services

Offset printed black and gray on
paler gray.

The John E. and Rhea Y. Fetzer Communications Media Center, an administrative unit of Upjohn Library, is the media service center for the entire college community. The primary emphasis of the center is to support the academic program.

Location

The center is located in suite 212 of Dewing Hall. Telephone: 383-8417.

Facilities

The center's facilities include an instructional media and equipment distribution center, an audio lab, video and graphics design studios, a darkroom for black and white film processing, a photography area, and a repair shop.

Hours

The center is open Monday through Friday from 8:00 a.m. to 5:00 p.m. Summer and holiday hours may vary.

Film/Video Ordering

Films and videotapes for both academic and administrative use are ordered and scheduled by the center staff. To assure availability, requests are due no later than the ninth week of the quarter preceding the scheduled showing. A collection of media resource information is maintained at the center to assist users in identifying appropriate media titles.

Consultation/Workshop Services

The center staff offers professional consultation and workshop services. It is committed to active collaboration with faculty and students in the design and selection of appropriate materials for teaching and learning.

Equipment Distribution

The Fetzer Media Center is responsible for the daily distribution of audiovisual equipment for classes, administrative events, and college-sponsored community functions. With prior scheduling, media center personnel will deliver, set up, and operate equipment. The following equipment is available for use:

- 8mm camera, projector
- 16mm projectors
- overhead projectors
- opaque projector
- record players
- cassette and reel-to-reel audiotape recorders
- slide projectors
- screens
- 35mm camera
- video equipment (for video class use only)
- portable light kits

Equipment Loan Period

Equipment can be signed out during regular office hours. If needed after 5:00 p.m. or on the weekend, equipment must be picked up between 4:00 and 5:00 p.m. of the work day immediately prior to its use and is due at 8:00 a.m. the following work day. Training is given as needed. Borrowers are responsible for the proper care and prompt return of all equipment.

Graphics/Photography

The Fetzer Media Center provides copystand, slide duplication, and limited black and white photographic services for faculty and students. Original graphics work, charts, signs, and overhead transparencies are prepared for instructional and research purposes and for other college-wide activities. A minimum of one week is required for graphics and photographic requests; instructional requests are given priority. To meet deadlines, please plan well in advance.

Public Address Systems

The staff maintains and operates public address systems for special events in Dalton Theatre, the Recital Hall, Stetson Chapel, Old Welles Hall, the Round Room, the Olmsted Room and occasionally in other areas of the college. A reservation form, available in the media center and in the Stetson Chapel office, must be submitted at least two weeks in advance of a scheduled event.

THE JOHN E. AND RHEA Y. FETZER
COMMUNICATIONS MEDIA CENTER

The John E. and Rhea Y. Fetzer Communications Media Center is the media service center for the entire college community. The Center emphasizes services to the academic program and is an administrative unit of the Upjohn Library.

LOCATION

The Center is located in **suite 212 of Dewing Hall**. Its facilities include a film and equipment distribution center, audio lab, small video studio, graphic design studio, black and white darkroom, small photography area, and a small repair shop.

HOURS

Monday through Friday from 8:00 a.m. to 5:00 p.m. (Summer and holiday hours may vary.)

SERVICES OF THE CENTER

Video Production

The Media Center offers a variety of video services. All video requests should be scheduled through the Media Center. Playback capability (3/4" videocassette decks and 1/2" VHS standard play decks) is currently available in Dewing Hall, Upjohn Library, the Light Fine Arts Building, Anderson Athletic Center, Mandelle Hall, Hicks Center, and the Stryker Center. The Media Center also offers video critique sessions on a limited basis for classroom use when arrangements have been made by faculty during the quarter preceding the taping. The Media Center tapes programs off-the-air for faculty in compliance with copyright guidelines. Briefly stated, they are:

A program may be videotaped simultaneously as broadcast at the request of an individual. Programs may not be taped routinely in anticipation of request(s).

The taped program may then be shown once for classroom use and can be retained for 45 calendar days (evaluation purposes).

Audio Production

The Media Center's audio lab is responsible for duplicating and recording audiotapes for language classes and College events. Additionally, the Media Center trains music recordists and transfers records and reel to reel audiotape recordings to cassettes for archival and individual use. The Language Lab in Dewing Hall is equipped with audio carrels and is maintained by the Center staff.

Graphics/Photography

The Media Center provides copystand and slide duplication services to students and faculty with a minimum of one week's notice. The Media Center offers limited black and white photographic services as well. Original graphic work is available for instructional and research purposes as well as for other college-wide activities. Graphics requests require a minimum of one week. Instructional requests take priority. In order to meet deadlines, please plan graphics well in advance.

Public Address Systems

The staff maintains and operates public address systems for special events in Dalton, the Recital Hall, Stetson Chapel, Old Welles, the Round Room, Olmsted, and occasionally in other areas as well. An "In-House Reservation" form should be filled out a few weeks in advance of the event detailing all pertinent information. These forms are available in the Media Center and in the Chapel Office.

Equipment Distribution

The Media Center is responsible for the daily distribution of audiovisual equipment to classrooms, administrative events, and college-sponsored community functions. The following equipment is available for use:

> 8mm camera, projector
> 16mm projectors
> overhead projectors
> opaque projector
> record players
> audiotape recorders - cassette
> audiotape recorders - reel to reel
> slide projectors
> screens
> 35mm camera
> video equipment (limited to video class use only)
> portable light kits

If scheduled in advance, the Media Center personnel will deliver, set up, and serve as operators of equipment if needed. After hours equipment must be picked up between 4:00 and 5:00 p.m. the day of use and is due at 8:00 a.m. the next morning. Borrowers are responsible for all equipment checked out in their name.

Film/Video Ordering

The Media Center actively orders and schedules film and video for academic and administrative use. Film and video orders are due the ninth week of the preceding quarter to assure availability. A variety of resource information is available at the Media

Center for faculty interested in researching appropriate media titles and subject matter. Funds for rental of audiovisual software are allocated to the Media Center budget. The Coordinator will work closely with departmental chairpersons to determine the needs within the budget.

Consultation/Workshop Services

The staff of the Fetzer Media Center offers ongoing consultation and workshop services and is committed to active collaboration with faculty and students to design and select appropriate techniques for teaching and learning.

Fees

The Media Center charges the instructional user for supply costs only. There is a fee schedule for non-instructional units of the College and for community groups. Please check with the Coordinator of the Fetzer Media Center for the current fee schedule.

COPYRIGHT POLICY FOR DUPLICATING
NON-PRINT MEDIA

V. Duplication of Non-Print Media

C. Guidelines for off-air recording of broadcast
programming for educational purposes. (Congressional
Record, October 14, 1981, pp. E 4750-E 4752.)

1. The guidelines were developed to apply only to
off-air recordings by non-profit education
institutions.

2. A broadcast program may be recorded off-air
simultaneously with broadcast transmission
(including simultaneous cable retransmission) and
retained by a non-profit educational institution
for a period not to exceed the first forty-five
(45) consecutive calendar days after date of
recording. Upon conclusion of such retention
period, all off-air recordings must be erased or
destroyed immediately. "Broadcast programs" are
television programs transmitted by television
stations for reception by the general public
without charge.

3. Off-air recording may be used once by individual
teachers in the course of relevant teaching
activities, and repeated once only when
instructional reinforcement is necessary, in
classrooms and similar places devoted to
instruction within a single building, cluster or
campus, as well as the homes of students receiving
formalized home instruction, during the first ten
(10) consecutive school days in the forty-five
(45) calendar day retention period. "School days"
are school session days -- not counting weekends,
holidays, vacations, examination periods, or other
scheduled interruptions -- within the forty-five
(45) calendar day retention period.

4. Off-air recordings may be made only at the request
of and used by individual teachers, and may not be
regularly recorded in anticipation of requests.
No broadcast program may be recorded off-air more
than once at the request of the same teacher,
regardless of the number of times the program may
be broadcast.

5. A limited number of copies may be reproduced from each off-air recording to meet the legitimate needs of teachers under these guidelines. Each such additional copy shall be subject to all provisions governing the original recording.

6. After the first ten (10) consecutive school days, off-air recordings may be used up to the end of the forty-five (45) calendar day retention period only for teacher evaluation purposes, i.e., to determine whether or not to include the broadcast program in the teaching curriculum, and may not be used by the recording institution for student exhibition or any other non-evaluation purpose without authorization.

7. Off-air recordings need not be used in their entirety, but the recorded programs may not be altered from their original content. Off-air recordings may not be physically or electronically combined or merged to constitute teaching anthologies or compilations.

8. All copies of off-air recordings must include the copyright notice on the broadcast program as recorded.

9. Education institutions are expected to establish appropriate control procedures to maintain the integrity of these guidelines.

D. Permissible uses of prerecorded and videotapes (home videotape rental stores).

1. Teachers and pupils are exempt under Title 17, Section 110 (1) to perform copyrighted works in face-to-face instruction, with the following limitations.

   a. The performance is part of a systematic course of instruction and not for entertainment, recreation, or cultural value.

   b. Attendance at performances is limited to pupils enrolled in the course, and to their teacher(s).

   c. The performance is given in a classroom or a similar place devoted to instruction, including libraries and gymnasiums, so long as the attendance limitation (Item B, above) is satisfied.

d.   The performance is given from a **legitimately-**made copy, which was not sold under a license or contract restricting school performances.

FETZER COMMUNICATION MEDIA CENTER CHARGING SCHEDULE   6/88

Equipment Rental Fees	On-Campus Non-Instructional	Off-Campus Guest
16 mm projector & screen	$8.00	$15.00
Projectionist	$3.60/hour	$3.60/hour
Video deck & monitor (3/4" Dewing & Upjohn Library) (1/2" Dewing only)	$8.00	$15.00
Slide projector & screen	$5.00	$10.00
Overhead & screen	$5.00	$10.00
Screen only	$1.00	$2.00
Video projector (D103 only)	$10.00	N/A

Public Address Set-ups		
Dalton, D103	$3.60	$10.00 + $5.00 each additional mic.
Old Welles, Round Room, Stetson	$7.20	$10.00 + $5.00 each additional mic.
President's Lounge, PDR	$10.00	$10.00 + $5.00 each additional mic.
Olmsted Room - 1 microphone	$3.60	$10.00
Olmsted Room - multiple mics.	$7.20	+ $5.00 each add. mic.

*Audio Services		
High-speed duplication	free	not available
Real-time duplication	$3.60/hour	not available
Editing	$3.60/hour	not available

*Video Services		
Studio set-up	$15.00 + $10.00/hour	not available
Field (remote) set-up	$20.00 + $10.00/hour	not available

*Graphics Services		
Photography		
Copystand (per exposure)	$1.00	not available
Slide duplication (per exposure)	$1.00	not available
Studio shot	by the job	not available
Field shot	by the job	not available
Darkroom/processing/enlargements	ask for current prices	not available
Original artwork	by the job	not available
Signs		
Lettering	$ .60/line	not available
Print press	$1.00/per sign	not available

*Prices do not include cost of materials (film, video & audio tapes, poster board etc.)

107

MOUNT SAINT MARY'S COLLEGE

Mount Saint Mary's College
Emmitsburg, Maryland 21727-7799

TO: All Faculty, Staff, and Administrators
FROM: Dr. John R. Popenfus, Director of Media Services
DATE: August 17, 1989
SUBJECT: COPYRIGHT LAW GUIDELINES
Multi-Media Center

The following is a brief and informative outline covering copyright law.
If there is something more you need to know or if you have questions
regarding this material, please contact the Media Center. You may save
this material for a reference guide throughout the coming school year.
Additional copies will be available.

I. Written Material

A. You May:

    1. Copy the following for lesson preparation or research (1 copy)

        a. chapter of a book
        b. article from a periodical or newspaper
        c. short story or essay
        d. short poem

    2. Make multiple copies for classroom use IF:

        a. it is "inspirational" - not enough time to expect a timely
            reply to a request for permission   AND
        b. a complete poem, if under 250 words   OR
        c. an excerpt from a longer poem, not to exceed 250 words   OR
        d. a complete article, story or essay of less than 2500
            words or 10% of the whole, whichever is less (2500 words
            maximum)   OR
        e. a chart, graph, diagram, drawing, cartoon, or picture,
            limited to one such illustration per book or periodical
            issue   AND
        f. the copying is for one course only   AND
        g. one work from a single author and no more than 3 authors
            from a collective work   AND
        h. no more than 9 instances of "inspirational" copying in
            one school term   AND
        i. the original copyright notice must appear on all copies
            of the work   AND
        j. you must follow the above guidelines completely if you
            do "inspirational" copying
        k. you must write for permission when the copying is NOT
            spontaneous
            i.   you may use the material until you have an answer
            ii.   if the answer is "No," then all copies MUST be
                  destroyed at that time
            iii. if copy permission is granted, you may have further
                  criteria to meet (such as a charge from the publisher)
                  and must do so
            iv.   by writing for permission, they may grant you permission
                  even if you do not meet all of the above criteria (b-i)

111

I. Written Material - continued

  B. You May Not:

    1. Copy to create or to replace or substitute for anthologies, compilations or collective works

    2. Copy an entire work

      a. unless for research ONLY   __AND__
      b. the original work is not available for purchase

    3. Reuse a copyright permission

      a. 1 time application
      b. may not use for the same class next year

    4. Copy consumable works, eg. workbooks and standardized tests

    5. Charge student beyond the actual cost of the photocopying

      a. you may pass on any charge to the student that was incurred from obtaining the copyright permission

    6. Out of print does NOT give you permission to photocopy

  C. The above rights to reproduction do NOT apply to

    1. Musical works

      a. see the Media Center for further information

    2. Pictorial, graphic, or sculptural works

    3. Motion picture or other audio-visual works

II. Audio-Visual Materials

  A. You May:

    1. Record off-air to video tape:

      a. for educators only   __AND__
      b. may use once in class for instructional purpose (once more is allowed for reinforcement) within 10 school days __AND__
      c. may hold for personal reference for 45 calendar days __AND__
      d. may only record once for the same teacher (fall & spring recordings NOT allowed) __AND__
      e. multiple copies may be made
        i. to meet legitimate needs of teachers
        ii. each additional copy is subject to the above provisions __AND__
      f. the tape need not be used in its entirety, but the program may not be altered, combined, or merged __AND__
      g. all copies of off-air recordings must include the copyright notice on the broadcast program as recorded __AND__
      h. the Media Center has the required control procedures established to maintain the integrity of these guidelines __OR__
      i. you may obtain a license to tape off-air (and keep the tape) for a fee - PBS does this often __OR__
      j. you may purchase a "For Home Use Only" video and show it in class if you are present in the class for instructional purposes only

II. Audio-Visual Materials - continued

    B. You May Not:

        1. Tape off-air at home and bring to school for class use

            a. unless the above guidelines are met   <u>AND</u>
            b. you bring the tape into the Media Center

        2. <u>Rent</u> a video to show in class

            a. unless you have <u>written</u> permission from your rental agency
            b. even then, this <u>is a</u> "gray area" - it has not been court
               tested and could be construed as illegal

    C. Closed Circuit Broadcasts

        1. Instructional films only

        2. Must be seen with teacher present

        3. Within one building only - not multiple buildings

        4. Check for limitations of broadcast with the company you
           purchased from

            a. they may charge extra for transmission

    D. Audio Material (Music)

        1. May NOT be taped off-air

        2. Background music for presentations

            a. allowed for students
            b. NOT allowed for instructors

        3. May NOT copy from one medium to another (album to cassette, etc.)

III. When In Doubt:

    A. Write for permission

    B. Seek help from the Media Center

        1. For interpretation of copyright law

        2. Finding copyright holder

        3. Obtaining copyright permissions

    C. Ignorance is NOT an excuse

    D. The following fines apply for copyright violations per each
       infraction

        1. $250.00 minimum - $10,000.00 maximum fine

        2. 1 - 2 year prison term

        3. May also be accompanied by a civil suit

III. When In Doubt: - continued

    E.. Who is liable?

        1. The institution (Mount Saint Mary's College)

        2. The Board of Trustees

        3. The instructor (You)

        4. The Media Specialist (Media Center personnel, print shop, etc)

        5. Book Store personnel

IV. Permission to copy letter should include:

    A. Title

    B. Author

    C. Publisher (Producer), Year

    D. Portions to be copied (lines, pages, segments)

    E. Number of copies

    F. Distribution Intent (Course title)

    G. Person requesting (Instructor's name)

    H. A copy of copyright page

Let the Media Center help you. Let the Media Center protect you.
Please follow the above guidelines and if you're not sure or what
you need is not covered, please contact us at extensions 4280 or 4360.

NAZARETH COLLEGE OF ROCHESTER

Photoduplicated, with pages of a
variety of pastel colors.

MEDIA BULLETIN CONTENTS

GENERAL INFORMATION

The Media Center is located on the lower level of the Lorette Wilmot Library, and is open the same hours as the library. There is a media software desk, office, playback area, self-help duplication area, media production facilities, viewing rooms, and the microcomputer lab.

The Media Software collection contains a growing assortment of tapes, compact discs, videotapes, slides, computer software and other materials. Most materials are used in the library on playback equipment. Media materials may also be used by faculty and students for classroom presentations.

The library's collection can be accessed through the LS2000 online catalog. The LS2000 online catalog terminals are located opposite the Media Software desk. Instructions are located at the terminals and staff members are available to help.

The microcomputer area consists of a microcomputer classroom with eight Apple computers, monitors, and printers. This room can be reserved for classes as well as for individual use. The microcomputer lab area consists of 2 Apple IIGS and 7 Macintosh computer set-ups. These may be reserved for individual use only.

MEDIA SOFTWARE DESK

Monday-Thursday	8 a.m.- midnight
Friday	8 a.m.- 10 p.m.
Saturday	10 a.m.- 10 p.m.
Sunday	12 p.m.- midnight

MEDIA OFFICE HOURS

Monday-Thursday	8 a.m.- 10:30 p.m.
Friday	8 a.m.- 5 p.m.
Saturday	10 a.m.- 2:30 p.m.
Sunday	12 noon-3:30 p.m.

HOLIDAY AND VACATION HOURS MAY VARY.
CHECK THE LIBRARY FOR HOURS.

MEDIA CENTER STAFF

Lori Widzinski	ext. 463	Director of Media Services
Sue Atkins	ext. 460	Media Office Coordinator
Kathy Marlin	ext. 459	Media Equipment Manager
Beth Sutter	ext. 466	Media Production Specialist
Mary Van Keuren	ext. 460	Media Evening Supervisor
Jeanette Peer	ext. 460	Media Evening Supervisor
Bill Eggers	ext. 449	Media Technical Assistant

1

MEDIA OFFICE SERVICES

If you are unable to find the particular film or video tape you need for your class among our collection, you can use our rental and preview services. The Media Center staff will assist you in locating desired titles.

RENTALS: 16mm films and video cassettes may be obtained from a wide variety of places for varying rental fees. Some local agencies are: The Rochester Public Library, and the RRLC (Rochester Regional Library Council) . If the material is not available locally it can be obtained from other college and commercial distributors.

Orders may be placed by phone or by making out a media request form at the Media Center Office. The Media Center will schedule, receive and return all films requested through the Media Center.

PLEASE ORDER WELL IN ADVANCE. ALLOW A MINIMUM OF 2 WEEKS FOR LOCAL BOOKINGS AND 3 WEEKS FOR COMMERCIAL BOOKINGS.

PREVIEWS: The Media Center can arrange for previews of a large variety of commercial software. Media rooms may be reserved for screenings.

MEDIA ROOMS: The following rooms are available for faculty and students to use for viewing software. They may be reserved by telephone or by stopping by the Media Office. Again, PLEASE RESERVE ROOMS AS EARLY AS POSSIBLE to insure you get the room you want.

MEDIA C: A small previewing room equipped with table and wall screen. Seats 2.

MEDIA D: Classroom equipped with large screen TV, 1/2" and 3/4" video players, overhead projector, wall screen and blackboard. Seats 30.

MEDIA E: Classroom equipped with large screen TV, 1/2" and 3/4" video players, 16mm projectors, slide projector, overhead projector, wall screen and blackboard. Seats 50.

2

RARE BOOK ROOM: Located on the main floor, has large conference
                   table and markerboard. Seats 15.

MICROCOMPUTER
   CLASSROOM: Contains 8 Apple computers with printers,
                   blackboard, overhead projector, and wall screen.
                   Seats 25.

MICROCOMPUTER
        LAB: This room cannot be reserved for classes; it is
                   an open lab. It houses 7 Macintosh computers
                   with Imagewriter printers, and 2 Apple IIGS
                   computers with printers and music boards.

MEDIA EQUIPMENT: If you need media equipment for your class, make
                        arrangements through the media office. Please allow
                        24 hours advance notice.

SLIDE DUPLICATION: Copies of slides can be arranged through the Media
                          Office. The slides are processed off campus, and
                          require one week turn-around time. Cost is 40 cents
                          per slide for the first copy, 25 cents per slide for
                          additional copies of the same slide.

☞ *FOR FURTHER INFORMATION, CONTACT SUE ATKINS, EXT. 460.*

3

MEDIA SOFTWARE DESK SERVICES

The Media Software Desk provides several services for library patrons.

SOFTWARE LOANS: Students may check out cassette tapes and graphics for use outside the library. All other software (records, videos films, filmstrips, computer software, etc.) is restricted to library use only. Faculty may check out all types of software.

RESERVE MATERIALS: Media software placed on reserve is restricted to library use only. The materials are arrranged in alphabetical order by the last name of the instructor, in the small file drawers located at the Media Software Desk. Faculty members placing material on reserve must fill out a Reserve Request Form, which are available in the Media Office. Please allow a two day processing time for materials placed on reserve.

MICROCOMPUTER RESERVE: The microcomputers in the lab must be signed out at the Media Software Desk. Computers may be reserved for 2 HOURS a day. Reservations will not be held longer than 1/2 hour.

TYPING ROOMS: Four typing rooms are equipped with electric typewriters and work tables. Rooms are reserved at the Media Software Desk. There is no time limit on typing room reservations.

PURCHASES: A variety of media supplies can be purchased at the Media Software Desk. For a complete list, see page 10.

FINES: Fines are five cents per day with a $5.00 maximum penalty.

4

COPIES:

XEROX: Paper copies can be made on the Xerox copiers across from the Media Software Desk. Both letter size and legal size paper is available on the lower level. Reductions in copy size can also be made. Copies are 5 cents each. Cards may be purchased in $5.00 denominations for use with the card-op device located on the copiers.

MICROFORM: Microfilm and microfiche copies can be made at the Media Software Desk. Copies are 5 cents each and the machines are patron operated. Assistance is available at the Media Software Desk if needed.

LASER PRINTING: An Apple Laserwriter and a Macintosh 512K Enhanced microcomputer are located near the Media Software Desk. Patrons may print out material saved on their own disks. The cost is 10 cents per page and assistance is available at the Media Software Desk.

☞ *FOR MORE INFORMATION, CONTACT SUE ATKINS, EXT. 460.*

5

EQUIPMENT DELIVERY

The following media equipment is available for classroom use and may be ordered from the Media Center by phone or by stopping by the Media Center Office: Monday-Friday, 8 a.m.-10:30 p.m.; Saturday,10 a.m.-2:30 p.m.

PROJECTORS	AUDIO/VIDEO	OTHER
8mm Film	Audio Cassette Recorders	Calculators
16mm Film	Reel to Reel Recorders	Portable Screens*
Slide	Record Players	35mm Camera
Slide Sound	Portable P.A.	Copy Stand
Filmstrip Record	1/2"Video Cassette Recorders	Apple Computer
Filmstrip Silent	3/4"Video Cassette Recorders	Leading Edge-
Filmstrip Cassette	Reel to Reel B/W Video Recorder	Computer
Microfiche	Beta II,III Recorder	Computer
Overhead*	Portable Color Video Cameras	Projection panel
Opaque	Videodisc Player	
	Compact Disc Player	
	Microphones	

*Smyth Hall, Arts Center & Shults Center have been equipped with Screens, Overheads and Carts.

PLEASE REQUEST EQUIPMENT AT LEAST
24 HOURS IN ADVANCE OF USE DATE.

All equipment will be set up for you and picked up after your class. Please notify us if equipment is inoperative, and we will try to replace it immediately. If you have a last minute request, you are welcome to pick up the equipment yourself at the equipment counter in the Media Office. Operators are available if requested ONE WEEK in advance.

Media equipment set-ups are available to non-affiliated groups using the Nazareth Campus for a fee. Audiovisuals are $10 per set up. **We would appreciate a minimum 10 day advance notice**. A projectionist or operator is available for the following fee:

Monday- Friday:	8:30 a.m.-4:00 p.m.	$8.00/hour (min. 2 hr.)
	4:00 p.m.-10:00 p.m.	$12.00/hour (min. 3 hr.)
Weekends:	as requested, $15.00/hour (min. 2 hours)	

These charges are for "normal" audiovisual needs and requests. Any "special requests" will be charged according to need and services requested. Priority for equipment is given to the College's academic needs and requirements.

☞*FOR ALL EQUIPMENT REQUESTS CALL KATHY MARLIN, EXT. 459.*

6

MEDIA PRODUCTION SERVICES

A wide range of production services is available for students, faculty and staff. In most cases, there is only a charge for the materials used. See price list pg. 10. Please make arrangements for production work as far in advance as possible. The following services are available:

VIDEO PRODUCTION:

VIDEO RECORDING: Single or multi-camera recordings of class lectures, guest speakers or special events.

MULTIPLEXING: 16mm and 8mm films, 35mm slides may be transferred to a video tape.

OFF-AIR RECORDING: Television programs may be copied off-air at the request of a faculty member and in compliance with copyright guidelines. Programs taped off-air can be retained for 45 days, after which they must be erased unless copyright clearance has been obtained.

VIDEO DUPLICATION: 1/2", 3/4", and Beta II, III video cassettes may be duplicated, in accordance with copyright restrictions.

EDITING, DUBBING, TITLING: Special program development and assistance is available. PLEASE MAKE ARRANGEMENTS AS FAR IN ADVANCE AS POSSIBLE.

AUDIO PRODUCTION:

AUDIO RECORDING: Reel-to-reel and stereo cassette recording equipment is available for recording classroom activity or special events.

DUPLICATIONS: Upon request, both reel-to-reel and cassettes may be duplicated.

OFF-AIR RECORDING: Local AM or FM stations may be recorded upon request and in compliance with copyright guidelines and staff availability.

PHOTOGRAPHY AND
GRAPHICS PRODUCTION:

THERMOFAX
DUPLICATION: Transparencies and laminating film are
                   available.

35MM PHOTOGRAPHY: Copystand duplications with a 35mm camera and
                   macro lens services available. Allow 2-3 weeks.

3M LETTERING
SYSTEM: Creates type on tape for labels, mechanicals,
                   posters, etc. A variety of typestyles and sizes
                   are available at the media software desk.

SLIDE PRODUCTION: Slides can be produced for the price of 40 cents
                   per slide; 25 cents for each additional copy.

LETERON LETTERS: Machine punched press on letters, ideal for posters
                   and signs. Many colors and sizes available. Inquire
                   at the Media Office.

CANON COLOR   Full color copies can be made with our new Canon
LASER COPIES: Color Laser Copier. A variety of special
                   effects can be achieved. Three paper sizes and
                   transparencies are available. See price list page.

SIGN DESIGN: We can design simple signs or flyers that can be
                   duplicated on a copier or be prepared for printing.
                   Allow 2-3 weeks. May be limited by availability
                   of materials.

DRY MOUNT PRESS: For mounting or laminating larger pieces.

NOTE: *THE MEDIA CENTER COMPLIES WITH ALL COPYRIGHT REGULATIONS AND
GUIDELINES AND RESERVES THE RIGHT TO REFUSE REQUESTS IN CONFLICT WITH
COPYRIGHT LAW.*

*FOR MORE INFORMATION OR TO MAKE ARRANGEMENTS FOR MEDIA
PRODUCTION SERVICES, CALL BETH SUTTER, EXT. 466.*

8

SELF-HELP DUPLICATION AREA

There is a self-help duplication area located just outside the Media Office. Patrons may use the machines themselves to produce the various types of media materials available. Instructions on use are posted by all machines. Media Center staff will be happy to help you if needed. Patrons may pay for supplies at the Media Software Desk.

THERMOFAX MACHINE: Students, faculty & staff can make ditto masters, laminations, and transparencies in a variety of colors on the Thermofax machine.

CASSETTE DUPLICATION: The stereo cassette-to-cassette duplicator will copy one cassette at a time, both sides of the cassette simultaneously. Blank tapes are available at the Media Software Desk.

STEREO CONSOLE: Located in the Media Playback Area is a high quality stereo console. Stereo reel-to-reel tapes may be transferred to cassette, as well as records and cassette recordings transferred to reel-to-reel. Obtain a set of headphones for listening at the Media Software Desk.

3M LETTERING MACHINE: Various type sizes and styles are available for signs, posters, etc. The letters are 5 cents per inch. A sample of available type fonts and sizes follows on pg. 12.

THE COPYRIGHT LAW OF THE UNITED STATES (TITLE 17 U.S. CODE) GOVERNS THE REPRODUCTION OF COPYRIGHTED MATERIAL. THE PERSON USING THIS EQUIPMENT IS LIABLE FOR ANY INFRINGEMENT.

9

MEDIA SERVICES AND SUPPLIES LIST

CANON COLOR LASER COPIES:	PRICE

NAZARETH AFFILIATED

-8 1/2 x 11	$.95
-11 x 17	$1.50
-Transparency	$ 2.00

NON-NAZARETH:

-8 1/2 x 11	$3.00
-11 x 17	$4.00
-Transparency	$5.00

THERMOFAX MATERIALS

TRANSPARENCIES	$.50
-black on clear	
-black on color	
-color on clear	

LAMINATING SHEETS	$.50

SPIRIT MASTERS	$.50

TRANSPARENCY SUPPLIES

-OH pens	$.75
-Frames	$.50

SLIDE MATERIALS	$.10

black-out slides, paper mounts,
write-on slides, plastic mounts,
Kaiser (Wess) mounts

Continued. . .

10

AUDIO CASSETTE TAPES   PRICE

PRICE INCLUDES CASE AND LABELS IF DESIRED.

C-30	$1.00
C-45	$1.25
C-60	$1.50
C-90	$2.00

STUDIO MASTER CHROME TAPE

(RECOMMENDED FOR BETTER QUALITY MUSIC RECORDINGS)

C-60	$2.50
C-90	$3.00

AUDIO REEL TAPES

1200' reel	$6.00
1800' reel	$7.00

AMPEX REEL-TO-REEL AUDIO TAPE

(RECOMMENDED FOR MUSIC APPLICATIONS)

Series 406 (1.5 mil.) 2500'	$14.00
Series 407 (1.0 mil.) 3600'	$19.00

VIDEO TAPES

1/2" VIDEOCASSETTES (VHS)

30 min.	$5.00
60 min.	$5.50
90 min.	$6.00
2 hour	$6.50

HIGH GRADE :

60 min.	$6.00
2 hour	$7.00

3/4" VIDEOCASSETTES (U-MATIC)

30 min.	$12.00
60 min.	$13.00

REEL-TO-REEL VIDEOTAPE

1/2" reel, 80 min.	$20.00

COMPUTER DISKS

5 1/2" Disks	$2.00

3 1/2" Disks:

Double sided, double density	$2.00

11

3M LETTERING SYSTEM
CHOICE OF TYPEDISCS
.05¢ PER INCH

COMMERCIAL SCRIPT	MICROGAMMA BOLD ***
24 pt.	24 pt.
CLOISTER TEXT	OPTIMA
24 pt.	24 pt. 36 pt.
FLASH	OPTIMA SEMI BOLD
36 pt.	36 pt.
HELVETICA REGULAR ***	SOUVENIR MEDIUM
10 pt.	24 pt. 36 pt.
HELVETICA LIGHT	SOUVENIR BOLD
24 pt. 36 pt.	24 pt. 36 pt.
HELVETICA MEDIUM	STYMIE MEDIUM
18 pt. 24 pt. 36 pt.	24 pt.
HELVETICA MEDIUM *ITALIC*	STYMIE BOLD
18 pt. 24 pt. 36 pt.	24 pt.
HELVETICA BOLD	
24 pt.	

*** MUST USE MANUAL CONTROLS

12

Laminating Price List

	1 side	2 sides
3 x 12 =	0.25	0.50
8 1/2 x 11 =	0.50	1.00
11 x 17 =	1.00	2.00
22 x 30 =	3.50	7.50
37 x 52 =	9.75	19.50

$$\frac{width \times height}{2} \ (.01) = \$$$

[* round to nearest quarter]

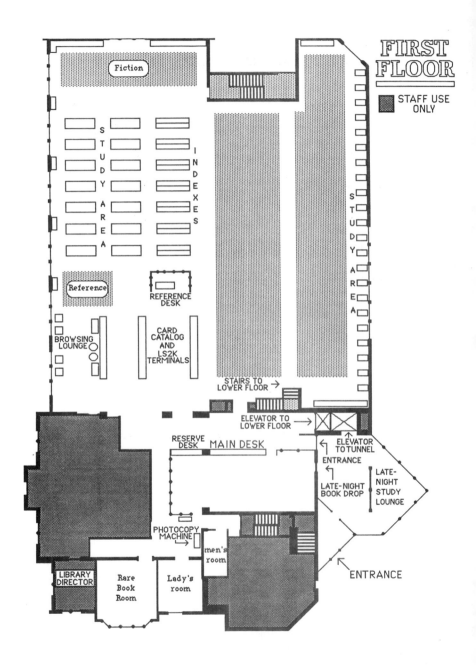

FIRST FLOOR

STAFF USE ONLY

Fiction

STUDY AREA

INDEXES

Reference

REFERENCE DESK

BROWSING LOUNGE

CARD CATALOG AND LS2K TERMINALS

STUDY AREA

STAIRS TO LOWER FLOOR →

ELEVATOR TO LOWER FLOOR →

RESERVE DESK   MAIN DESK

ELEVATOR TO TUNNEL

← ENTRANCE

← LATE-NIGHT BOOK DROP

LATE-NIGHT STUDY LOUNGE

PHOTOCOPY MACHINE →

men's room

LIBRARY DIRECTOR

Rare Book Room

Lady's room

ENTRANCE

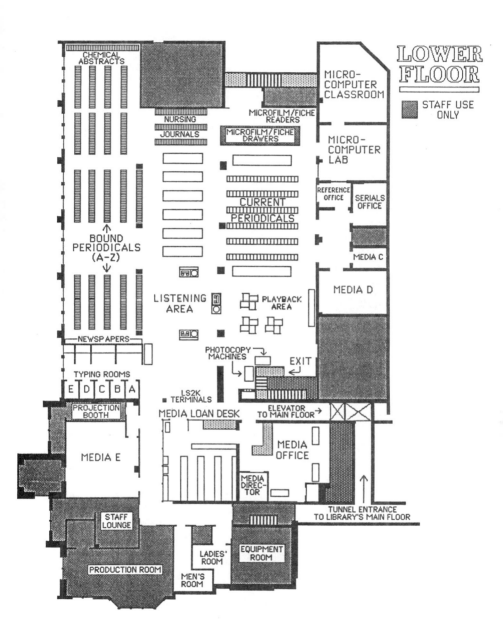

CHEMICAL ABSTRACTS

NURSING JOURNALS

MICROFILM/FICHE READERS

MICROFILM/FICHE DRAWERS

MICRO-COMPUTER CLASSROOM

MICRO-COMPUTER LAB

REFERENCE OFFICE

SERIALS OFFICE

CURRENT PERIODICALS

BOUND PERIODICALS (A-Z)

MEDIA C

MEDIA D

LISTENING AREA

PLAYBACK AREA

NEWSPAPERS

PHOTOCOPY MACHINES

EXIT

TYPING ROOMS

E D C B A

LS2K TERMINALS

PROJECTION BOOTH

MEDIA LOAN DESK

ELEVATOR TO MAIN FLOOR

MEDIA E

MEDIA OFFICE

MEDIA DIRECTOR

TUNNEL ENTRANCE TO LIBRARY'S MAIN FLOOR

STAFF LOUNGE

LADIES' ROOM

EQUIPMENT ROOM

PRODUCTION ROOM

MEN'S ROOM

LOWER FLOOR

STAFF USE ONLY

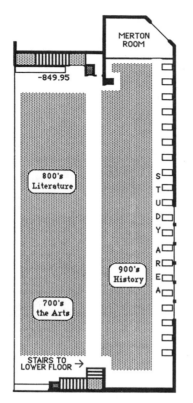

MEZZANINE

STAFF USE ONLY

NOTE: THERE IS NO ELEVATOR ACCESS TO THIS FLOOR.

MERTON ROOM

-849.95

800's
Literature

900's
History

700's
the Arts

STUDY AREA

STAIRS TO
LOWER FLOOR →

SIMPSON COLLEGE

FILM AND VIDEO RENTALS -- Simpson College

Currently, the cost of renting films or videos is charged to the supply line budget of the department which requested the rentals. The return postage is paid by the library. The library has no line item for rental costs.

Film and video rentals are usually handled through the Media Services office. Faculty members can chose films and/or videos through rental catalogs from the State Library, colleges, and companies. When a video is not available through the usual means, some faculty members chose to rent the video from a video store. In this case, the cost of renting videos is paid for by the faculty members themselves at a cost of $1.00 to $4.00 or is charged to their department.

Past inquiries about renting from video rental stores have come to the conclusion that this is legal only for home use, except in those instances where the video is used by teachers in their classrooms for the purpose of education (i.e. not entertainment). The following quote from A Viewer's Guide of Copyright Law explains this exemption:

"The following are not infringements of copyright: (1) performance or display of a work by instructors or pupils in the course of face-to-face teaching activities of a non-profit educational institution, in a classroom or similar place devoted to instruction, unless in the case of a motion picture or other audiovisual work the performance is given by means of a copy that was not lawfully made and that the person responsible for the performance knew or had reason to believe was not lawfully made".

If a faculty member decides to rent a video from a store, then they need to be aware that there is a fine line between the legal and illegal use of that video. If a video dealer asks the faculty member to sign an agreement that states the video will only be used at home, then the above exemption is no longer valid.

FILM AND VIDEO RENTALS -- Simpson College (cont.)

A Viewer's Guide of Copyright Law goes on to explain that in many cases it is best to use only those videos that have been cleared for public performance so there will be no legal questions. Simpson College does have a public performance contract with Films Incorporated that allows us to rent or purchase any video that is on their list (available at the Media Services office) and use it in a public setting. These videos do not necessarily have to be rented from Films Incorporated, but can be obtained from any video store or company.

An alternative to renting videos from stores would be to borrow them from public libraries. Indianola Public Library loans out their videos free-of-charge for one day and the Des Moines Public Library charges $0.50 for two days. Public library video lists are available at the Media Services office.

Gail Hiebert

Dunn Library
12-16-1988

138

The Copyright Law of 1976 gives the producers of a videotape the exclusive rights of distributing, displaying, adapting, copying and publicly showing a videotape. Dunn Library recognizes this copyright law and therefore will follow certain policies concerning the use of videotapes.

Videotapes in the collection that are checked out to faculty and staff may only be used in a classroom__situation, in a public performance_setting when the library has the license to show that particular title, or at home.

** Public performances of a videotape are considered any showing of the video to any groups of people outside the home. However, there is a classroom exemption that allows the showing of copyrighted videos to students in classroom situation. **

CLASSROOM EXEMPTION

** In order for the showing of a copyrighted video in a classroom to be legal certain requirements must be met: **

a_legally__made_copy__of_the__video (off-air videotapes can legally be shown if they are licensed or if they are shown within 10 days after their recording date)

must be shown_in_a_classroom or similar_place devoted_to_instruction (all campus teaching facilities meet this definition)

by__a__professor__or__a_student (face-to-face teaching situation)

and the video_must_be_curriculum_related (not merely shown for entertainment purposes)

(The classroom exemption from the copyright law does_not__apply_where the_videotape_was_not_lawfully_made and the person responsible either knew it was not or had reason to believe that it was not)

PUBLIC PERFORMANCES

If a videotape is to be shown outside of the classroom situation to a group, then the institution must have a public performance license for that particular video title in_order__for_the_showing to_be_legal. If the instituiton does not have such a license, the showing is illegal. The Media Services office has a list of the current videos/films for which Simpson College has a license.

>   ** Faculty that check out tapes for purposes other than classroom showings or home viewings will be asked to sign a form that states that they understand the limits of the copyright law and will be responsible for all liabilities. **

STUDENT VIEWING

If students miss a classroom showing of a video, they may set up a time with the Media Services office to watch the video. Students may watch videotapes from the Dunn Library collection in the library, but they may not check them out of the library. They will need to contact the Media Services office, between the hours of 8-5pm (M-F), to set up a viewing time.

OFF-AIR VIDEOTAPING

Programs that are broadcast on television can be recorded onto videotape for showing in the classroom situation, provided that this is done within ten days of the program's broadcast date. The Media Services office will do the recording at the request of a professor. This service is not offered to students. The person who requests the recording to be done must sign an off-air taping request form. These recordings may_be_kept_only_for__a_period_of 45_days, and they may_only_be_used_in_class_up_to_10_days_after the_time_they_were_recorded. If they are kept or shown beyond this specified time, then the recordings become illegal.

>   ** The Media Services office is willing to pick up the tapes after their expired time, erase them and have them available for use again thus saving an extra charge to the department for a new tape. **

COPYING

The duplication of any commercial videotapes in the Dunn Library collection violates the copyright law.

Information taken from:

   Stanek, Debra J. "Videotapes, Computer Programs,and the Library". Information_Technology_and__Libraries. March 1986. 42-54.
   Bender, Ivan. A_Viewer's_Guide_to_Copyright_Law:_What_Every School,_College_and_Public_Library_Should_Know. A.I.M.E., 1987.

SAMPLE FORM

I understand that this videotape is to be shown only in
the privacy of my own home or in a classroom, face-to-
face teaching situation. Any public performance
(showing this to a group of people outside the home or
classroom), would be violating the copyright law and I
would be held responsible.

Signature x_____

Date _____

DUNN LIBRARY
AUDIO-VISUAL EQUIPMENT
CHECK-OUT POLICY

The Media Services unit of Dunn Library exists to fulfill the audio-visual needs of the faculty, staff, and students of Simpson College. Guidelines for the use of college A/V equipment are outlined below. These policies are effective as of Monday, 23 May 1988.

1) A/V equipment may be checked out by Simpson faculty, staff, and students for use on the college campus. Community organizations meeting on campus may also borrow equipment with the signing of a statement of responsibility.

2) Faculty requests for off-campus instructional use of equipment will be considered in individual cases.

3) Students must have a sponsor in order to check out equipment. The sponsor may be a faculty member, a student development official, or the head resident of a housing unit. Sponsors accept responsibility for the authorized use of equipment. Those who actually use equipment are responsible for paying for damages due to negligence. Before students can check out A/V equipment, they must obtain their sponsor's signature on a form available in the Media Services office. The equipment will be released when the signed form is submitted to the Media Services Librarian.

4) Ordinarily, A/V equipment is checked out only for single class periods or events. Extensions may be negotiated if necessary. Some equipment may be checked out for an entire semester. Such requests will be honored as often as possible, subject to campus-wide demands for equipment.

5) Mechanical difficulties with A/V equipment should be immediately reported to the Media Services office, ext. 553. If the office cannot be contacted, a note describing the problem should be affixed to the protective case of the equipment before it is returned.

6) Equipment reservations should be made at least 48 hours in advance. Media Services cannot guarantee the availability of equipment ordered on shorter notice.

SWARTHMORE COLLEGE

SWARTHMORE

Swarthmore College Library

VIDEOCASSETTE CIRCULATION

* Videocassettes may circulate overnight after 4:00 p.m. to be returned by noon of the following day.

* Only two titles at a time may be taken out.

* Cassettes for classroom use may circulate at any time.

* Shakespeare and cassettes on reserve do not circulate with the exception of classroom use.

* Borrowers are liable for the full cost of the cassette plus a service charge if the cassette is not returned or is returned in an unviewable condition.

* Overdue fines are two dollars per day.

SWARTHMORE COLLEGE LIBRARY

LIBRARY VIDEO PROGRAM

The College Library has been acquiring videocassettes and playing equipment to support classroom instruction. The videocassette collection now amounts to some 900 titles mainly in the areas of English Literature (Shakespeare plays), theater, and cinema. The equipment is designed to accommodate half inch VHS cassettes and there is also one machine for three-quarter inch U-matic.

The Library encourages the use of its video equipment and cassettes in the areas set aside for this purpose in McCabe (Level IV). Facilities consist of:

1. A classroom to accommodate approximately 25 people. Use of this room by faculty for coursework should be scheduled with **Ann Blackburn X8489.**

2. A smaller room which can accommodate 4-6 people.

3. Individual viewing stations.

The Library's collection of videocassettes are available for general use; priority is always given to classroom instruction.

Videocassettes may be checked out after 4:00 p.m. to be returned by noon of the following day.

Overdue fines will be charged as for Reserve materials.

Videocassettes reserved for classroom instruction may not be borrowed.

If the material cannot be viewed in the Library equipment is available to faculty for classroom instruction. It is recommended that reservations be made at least 24 hours in advance of use. This equipment may not be borrowed for personal use.

The Library's videocassettes may not be copied, publicly exhibited, or used in any way that would violate copyright laws.

Hours of service:

Monday - Friday	1:00 - 5:00 p.m.; 7:00-11:45 p.m.
Saturday	1:00 - 5:00 p.m.
Sunday	1:00 - 5:00 p.m.; 7:00 - 11:45 p.m.

For further information contact **Ed Fuller** at **X8495**.

MJD:asb
12/22/89

TRINITY UNIVERSITY

AUDIOVISUAL ACQUISITIONS

IMS **PURCHASES** commercially produced audiovisual materials twice each year, in November and March. These purchases are based on faculty requests with priority given to material that will support more than one discipline. IMS also assists faculty in **BORROWING** or **RENTING** audiovisual materials for classroom use from off-campus sources. An extensive collection of indexes and commercial and university catalogues is available for faculty use in identifying the source and availability of audiovisual materials. In addition, Trinity is a member of the local library consortium, CORAL, whose members loan media resources to one another.

INSTRUCTIONAL MEDIA SERVICES

Fall and Spring Hours:

Monday-Thursday	8:00 a.m. - 10:00 p.m.
Friday	8:00 a.m. - 5:00 p.m.
Saturday	1:00 p.m. - 5:00 p.m.
Sunday	1:00 p.m. - 10:00 p.m.

Summer Hours:
Monday-Friday 8:00 a.m. - 5:00 p.m.

Phone Number: 736-7323
Maddux Library 4th Floor

4TH FLOOR MADDUX LIBRARY TRINITY UNIVERSITY

FACULTY COMMENTS

"Whether we like it or not, we now have a population of primarily visually literate students, and IMS represents a central and critical resource for tapping the full potential of their intellectual growth."
Dr. Larry Kimmel - Philosophy

"Audiovisuals are a relevant, even necessary, complement to the study of literature."
Dr. David Middleton - English

"IMS enables me to provide a richer classroom experience."
Dr. Char Miller - History

"IMS's services have strengthened my classroom presentations and national papers at little cost."
Dr. George Thompson - Business Administration

"In my opinion, learning must engage the senses and lead to reflection and action. Instructional Media Services are an integral part of my educational efforts at Trinity."
Dr. John Donahue - Sociology

MADDUX LIBRARY

August, 1987

WHAT'S BEHIND OUR DOORS?

Offset printed black on cream and tri-folded

CIRCULATION SERVICES

IMS **CIRCULATES** a collection of audiovisual materials, including videotapes, films, records, slides and filmstrips, for **student, faculty** and **staff** use. Audiovisual carrels are available for on-site use of all AV materials. IMS also maintains a Faculty Reserve where any type of AV material may be placed on semester reserve for specific classes.

MUSIC COLLECTION

The **MUSIC COLLECTION** is located in the IMS section of the library. This rapidly expanding collection is primarily classical music designed to support University courses; however, the library is beginning to purchase some popular and ethnic recordings. Music listening carrels are conveniently located for the use of these materials.

LANGUAGE LABORATORY

The **LANGUAGE LABORATORY** is also located in IMS. While the lab is designed for use by a complete class, with a teacher console and student booths, much of the use is on an individual basis. Students select their own audio cassette tapes from open shelves and proceed through the lessons at their own pace.

DISTRIBUTION SERVICES

IMS maintains an extensive inventory of audiovisual equipment for **DISTRIBUTION** campus-wide. This equipment can be checked out to faculty and staff, or can be delivered and operated by IMS staff. Equipment available includes slide, overhead, and 16mm projectors, audio and videotape recorders, and monitors. Most of this equipment is also available for student check-out with proper approval.

EQUIPMENT REPAIR

IMS **SERVICES** and **REPAIRS** all types of audiovisual and television equipment, with the exception of computer equipment. The costs for repairs to equipment owned by individual departments will be billed to the department.

CONSULTATION

IMS can **CONSULT** with faculty and staff on instructional media design, audiovisual equipment selection and specifications, planning and designing of instructional resources, and the design of media facilities for new construction and remodeling projects.

PRODUCTION SERVICES

IMS provides a complete range of audio and visual **PRODUCTION SERVICES** for faculty and staff. **PHOTOGRAPHIC** production includes slide duplication, color slides from flat copy, black-and-white negatives and prints, and on-location photography. **ART/GRAPHICS** production includes graphs, charts, line copy, and original artwork from your data or ideas, as well as creative ideas of our own to fit your needs. Graphic art for research publications or presentations is our specialty. **AUDIO/VIDEO** production includes on-location and studio taping as well as post-production editing, adding music and narration, duplication, and slide/tape synchronization.

OTHER SERVICES

A limited supply of new audio and video tapes, projection lamps, overhead transparency materials and other types of AV supplies are available for resale to departments not wishing to maintain an inventory of these items.

MEMORANDUM

TO: All Faculty Members

FROM: Ronnie C. Swanner, Instructional Media Services

DATE: February 15, 1989

SUBJECT: Audiovisual Material Purchases

Instructional Media Services is accepting requests from the
faculty for the purchase of commercially produced audiovisual
materials. If you are interested in the Library purchasing
any type of instructional material, please submit your request
to me by March 17, 1989. A request form is attached for your
use. All unfunded Fall Semester requests will be automatically
reconsidered for the Spring allocation. A list of the titles
purchased this Fall are attached.

If I can be of any assistance, please let me know.

Selection Crtieria

Any or all of the following criteria may be used in giving
priority consideration to requests for purchasing library materials.
However, requests which meet several of the criteria will generally take precedence.

Materials which:

Support more than one discipline,
Cannot be rented locally,
Are presently rented more than twice a year,
Will be used for several years,
Replace existing copies,
Can be purchased at a considerable discount, and
Support new faculty, courses, or areas of instruction.

Attachments

MADDUX LIBRARY
AV CIRCULATION POLICY

Regular Circulation

*Students -- All AV materials, including 3/4" video tapes (not VHS), slides,
films and phonograph records. Limit 3. Loan period: 3 days
with one renewal. Fine $1.00 per day.

Faculty/Staff -- All AV materials, including 3/4" video tapes (not VHS),
slides, films and phonograph records. Limit 3. Loan period:
3 days with one renewal. No fines.

Limited or Special Circualtion

Reserves

Audio/Visual material is placed on reserve at the IMS circulation
desk, except in special cases, according to the instructions of a
faculty member. Audio/Visual reserves rules are posted in the IMS
Department.

VHS Tapes
*Students - One day or over weekend with one renewal. Limit 1 overnight, 3
over the weekend. Fine $1.00 per day.

Faculty/Staff - One day or over weekend with one renewal. Limit 1 overnight,
3 over the weekend. No fines.

Music Recordings
Faculty - Loan period: 3 days with one renewal. Upon request for classroom
use, 1 semester. No limit. No fines.

Av Equipment
*Students - Certain AV equipment is available for instructional use. Requires
written permission from faculty member. Limit 3. Fine $1.00 per
day.

Faculty/Staff - Limited by availability only.

*Students are defined as persons currently enrolled at Trinity University and
taking one or more courses offered in the undergraduate/graduate class schedule.

Effective Date
January 12, 1987

Revised August 10, 1987